Grace to Lead

D1115441

Grace to Lead

Practicing Leadership in the Wesleyan Tradition

Kenneth L. Carder and Laceye C. Warner

General Board of Higher Education and Ministry
The United Methodist Church
Nashville, Tennessee

The General Board of Higher Education and Ministry leads and serves The United Methodist Church in the recruitment, preparation, nurture, education, and support of Christian leaders—lay and clergy—for the work of making disciples of Jesus Christ for the transformation of the world. Its vision is that a new generation of Christian leaders will commit boldly to Jesus Christ and be characterized by intellectual excellence, moral integrity, spiritual courage, and holiness of heart and life.

The General Board of Higher Education and Ministry of The United Methodist Church is the church's agency for educational, institutional, and ministerial leadership. It serves as an advocate for the intellectual life of the church. The Board's mission embodies the Wesleyan tradition of commitment to the education of laypersons and ordained persons by providing access to higher education for all persons.

Copyright 2011 by the General Board of Higher Education and Ministry, The United Methodist Church. All rights reserved.

No part of this book may be reproduced in any form whatsoever, print or electronic, without written permission, except in the case of brief quotations embodied in critical articles or reviews. For information regarding rights and permissions, contact the Office of Interpretation, General Board of Higher Education and Ministry, P.O. Box 340007, Nashville, TN 37203-0007; phone 615-340-7383; fax 615-340-7048. Visit our Web site at www.gbhem.org.

All Scripture quotations unless noted otherwise are taken from the *New Revised Standard Version of the Bible*, copyright 1989, Division of Christian Education of the National Council of Churches of Christ in the United States of America. Used by permission. All rights reserved.

Scripture quotations noted KJV are taken from the King James or Authorized Version of the Bible.

Scripture quotations marked ESV are taken from THE ENGLISH STANDARD VERSION. © 2001 by Crossway Bibles, a division of Good News Publishers.

ISBN 978-0-938162-76-6

Produced by the Office of Interpretation

Manufactured in the United States of America

Contents

Acknowledgments

The idea for writing a book on leadership from a Wesleyan perspective began when we team-taught a course for seminary students at Duke University Divinity School, titled Evangelism and Leadership in the Wesleyan Tradition. We set out to identify and appropriate insights from the eighteenth-century Wesleyan revival in England with the potential to motivate, form, and guide pastoral leaders in the twenty-first century. We are grateful to those students who became partners in the learning process and contributed their questions, vision, insights, and passion to the effort to learn from the early Methodists. We are also grateful for permission to draw from Warner's article "Spreading Scriptural Holiness: Theology and Practices of Early Methodism for the Contemporary Church," *The Asbury Journal* (Spring 2008), 115–38, which benefited greatly from conversations at the Twelfth Oxford Institute of Methodist Theological Studies in August 2007.

We are especially indebted to our colleagues at Duke Divinity School, who have contributed immeasurably to the growth in Wesley scholarship over the past thirty years. Ongoing dialogue with Edgardo Colon-Emeric, Stephen Gunter, Amy Laura Hall, Richard Heitzenrater, Greg Jones, Randy Maddox, and Joy Moore continue to enrich our understanding and deepen our insights. Conversation within the broader Duke Divinity School community, where the formation of pastoral leaders is at the core of our mission, provides fertile soil in which to grow in the understanding and the practice of Christian leadership. We are grateful to be part of such a community of learning and formation in which grace is more than an abstract theological concept.

Among the members of the Duke Divinity School community who have provided specific aid in the writing of this book are Rebecca Hymes-Smith, Judith Heyhoe, and Laura Levens. Rebecca's administrative support has been invaluable in creating the space and organization necessary for us to focus time on writing the manuscript. Judith's editorial skills helped to bring order and clarity to our thoughts and, while she cannot be faulted with the weaknesses of the final product, she significantly enhanced our efforts to provide a helpful resource for persons who seek to practice faithful Christian leadership. Laura brought to our efforts keen insights into connections between theory and practice and the formulation of questions that foster additional inquiry.

Introduction

Emerging Challenges and Opportunities
Require Principled Christian Leaders

Mainline denominations in the United States, including The United Methodist Church, stand at a crossroads. The church is poised between continuing decline in institutional viability and cultural influence and unparalleled opportunities for evangelical and missional engagement. Perhaps not since the apostolic age has the Christian church confronted such powerful social, political, and cultural currents as those swirling around it in the twenty-first century.

The church in the United States has been an integral part of the prevailing culture for more than two centuries. The United Methodist Church and its predecessors have enjoyed widespread support and influence within the broader population, and in the nineteenth century the Methodists were the fastest-growing and most visibly present denomination across the geographic landscape. Statistical growth, institutional vitality, and cultural influence were the norm; and church leadership consisted primarily of assimilating the growth, managing the church and its institutions, and preserving prevailing successful structures and strategies.

The current realities represent distinct challenges and call for different leadership. The disestablishment of mainline churches, religious pluralism, competing worldviews and ideologies, the power of the global market, and multiple societal forces now compete with the Christian church for determining values, vision, loyalties, and meaning. Global poverty and disease, the prevalence of war and violence, polarization within societies, and the longing for transcendent purpose, uniting vision, and unquenchable hope call forth the renewal of the church's witness and mission.

Throughout human history, God has called forth and equipped persons for the leadership needed in particular times and places. We are convinced that God provides what the church needs, and the church today needs leaders who are equipped to meet the exceptional challenges and opportunities of the present age. What is the source and character of principled Christian leaders? That is the question we address throughout this book.

Grace as Source, Motivation, and *Telos* of Christian Leadership

Christian leadership is a gift, not an achievement! It is grateful participation in the triune God's own life and mission in the world. Christian leadership begins, continues, and ends in *followership*, as we respond persistently through the power of the Holy Spirit to Jesus' invitation, "Come, follow me." As followers of Jesus Christ, we seek through the power of the Holy Spirit to do what he says to do, go where he leads, welcome those whom he loves and for whom he died, participate in the community he forms, and anticipate his final reign over all creation. Through friendship with Christ, we are formed as individuals and communities into signs, foretastes, and instruments of God's transformation of the world. We are shaped and formed in Christlikeness, led into avenues of service, placed in positions of influence, and empowered to be Christ's body in ministry in the world.

Leadership in the Christian community, therefore, is rooted in the triune God. It originates in *God the Father*, who creates us in the divine image with dignity, value, potential, purpose, and communion. It is derived in *God the Son*, who redeems us, incorporates us into the new creation, and claims us as his body. And Christian leadership is empowered by *God the Spirit*, who sustains us in community, empowers us to grow into Christlikeness, and calls us to live courageously and hopefully toward the final victory over the powers of sin and death.

Our Wesleyan heritage, with its central concept of *grace*, provides a framework for leadership formation in the church. Perhaps the following excerpt offers John Wesley's own definition of grace and its centrality in Christian life and leadership:

> *By "the grace of God" is sometimes to be understood that free love, that unmerited mercy, by which I, a sinner, through the merits of Christ am now reconciled to God. But in this place it rather means that power of God the Holy Ghost which "worketh in us both to will and to do of his good pleasure." As soon as ever the grace of God (in the former sense, his pardoning love) is manifested to our souls, the grace of God (in the latter sense, the power of his Spirit) takes place therein. And now we can perform through God, what to [ourselves] was impossible . . . a recovery of the image of God, as renewal of soul after His likeness.*[1]

The Wesleyan revival of the eighteenth century was motivated, shaped, and empowered by this robust and transformative understanding and experience of divine grace, which forgives, heals, and empowers individuals and communities. Although the cultural, political, and ecclesial realities of the twenty-first century vary significantly from those of the eighteenth, the leadership needs of contemporary "people called Methodists" are remarkably similar to those confronted by John and Charles Wesley and their colleagues in the movement.

While the Wesleyan revival included the development of institutions and drew on the skills of individuals and groups and intentional personal and organizational practices, the movement was propelled and shaped by an evangelical passion rooted and grounded in divine grace. It was Wesley's theological fervor and acumen, as expressed in his keen intellect and ardent commitment to holiness of heart and life, that shaped the methods and practices that characterized the movement. While he was adept at using the tools available in the broader culture, John Wesley steadfastly maintained his theological and missional focus throughout his long leadership of the Methodists. And divine grace—prevenient, justifying, and sanctifying—was the heart and soul of his theological and missional vision.

The implications for leadership of a lively and robust understanding of grace are immeasurable. Understood in the light of divine grace, leadership is a gift to be joyfully received and nurtured, rather than an achievement to be slavishly pursued. As grace, leadership emerges from friendship with the triune God— a living out of our identity as beloved, redeemed children of God, rather than a position to occupy or a profession to promote. Grace makes possible self-awareness, vulnerability, confession, forgiveness, and continuous growth, which are indispensable qualities of those who lead the church to be a herald and instrument of God's present and coming reign. Since grace is God's presence and power preceding our efforts, going before us and with us, Christian leadership is courageous and filled with hope.

Yearning for Leadership

The yearning for persons who will provide vision, motivation, and competency for society and its institutions is manifested in multiple ways within the church and broader society. Organizations decry the absence of quality leaders who can infuse energy and provide creative direction in a highly competitive environment, and efforts to address the need are mushrooming across the institutional landscape.

Leadership occupies growing attention throughout the world as institutions seek to preserve and enhance their viability and capacity in a rapidly changing environment. Leadership is proposed as the key to confronting the opportunities and challenges of the contemporary world. The failure of leadership ranks high on the lists of explanations for lost or diminished effectiveness of once-strong institutions; and analysts bemoan the widespread "leadership crisis" in today's world.

Strategies for filling the leadership void abound. Institutions devoted to identifying, forming, educating, and training persons as leaders are proliferating. *Leadership studies* have become a legitimate academic discipline in prestigious universities, and courses, seminars, and workshops are flourishing. A cursory search of the Internet indicates more than eight hundred thousand references to *leadership*. Books and articles on the subject are mushrooming. Amazon.com lists more than sixteen thousand full-length books on the topic, and numerous periodicals are dedicated to essays on the theme. Corporations, businesses, and agencies devote significant resources to enhancing the capacity and skills of their leaders.

The church reflects this preoccupation with leadership formation. Many denominational colleges, universities, and seminaries are forming institutes and strategies devoted to leadership formation. Denominational agencies are giving priority attention to programs and tactics directed toward calling forth, equipping, and supporting leaders for local churches and judicatories. Local congregations share society's yearning for strong leaders, including pastors and laity who can enable them to flourish and fulfill their mission; and considerable resources are earmarked for leadership recruitment and formation.

Leadership and the Christian Community

Defining and addressing leadership within the context of the Christian community represents particular challenges. As a social institution, the church faces the same needs, obstacles, and challenges in calling forth, forming, deploying, and sustaining those who lead congregations and other church-related institutions. The church can learn much from the social sciences and business world about leadership. However, the foundation, purpose, and meaning of leadership in the Christian community lie beyond the insights from social science. Christian communities must look for models of leadership in places other than the world of business and corporate America.

Christian leadership is defined, formed, and shaped by, as well as rooted and deployed in accordance with, who God is, where God is, what God is doing, and what God would have individuals and communities be and do. Leadership in the Christian community is a sharing in the life and mission of the triune God, which means that it begins, continues, and ends in communion with, obedience to, and praise of the God we know as Father, Son, and Holy Spirit. Such leadership is much more than institutional direction and management.

The *telos*, or ultimate end, of leadership within the Christian community is the reign of God, the increase in love of God and neighbor, and the transformation of individuals, communities, and the entire cosmos in response to God's redeeming and reconciling acts in creation, in history, and supremely in Jesus Christ. John Wesley, whom we acclaim as the founding leader of the Methodist movement, expressed the *telos* and mission of "the people called Methodist" in the Large Minutes: "What may we reasonably believe to be God's design in raising up the People called Methodists? A. To reform the nation and, in particular, the Church; to spread scriptural holiness over the land."[2] Leadership in the early Methodist movement was devoted to cultivating "holiness of heart and life" in individuals and communities as instruments of God's new creation.

Leadership in the church, therefore, may include a formalized office or position and involve particular functions and roles. Some church leaders are called upon to manage and direct organizations and institutions within and outside the church. But within the church, *being* and *character* precede *doing* and *skills*. *Theology* replaces anthropology and sociology as foundational; and vision and direction are determined by *divine mission* rather than by market consumerism. Personal and community transformation in response to God's reign of compassion, justice, generosity, and joy trumps institutional growth and self-fulfillment as the priority vision and purpose.

Without firm theological grounding in the church's mission as a sign, foretaste, and instrument of God's present and coming reign in Jesus Christ, the church's focus on leadership may be counterproductive or directed toward misguided or inadequate goals. It can result in a form of idolatry that supplants announcing the reign of God with enhancing the statistical growth of a church that has forgotten its mission. Leadership formation apart from Christian discipleship risks fostering qualities and values counter to Christian character and community—elitism and arrogance rather than solidarity and humility, personal achievement instead of faith formed by grace, manipulation rather than service, and competitiveness that fractures rather than nurtures community. Firm grounding in our Wesleyan theology and practice will enable us to maintain proper focus on the character and communal dimensions of Christian leadership.

Defining Leadership

While the emphasis on leadership is widespread in society, the academy, and the church, no consensus exists as to its definition, how it is called forth, what forms and shapes it, and how it is sustained. Leadership is most often identified as roles or positions of authority within institutions. Leaders are identified as chief executive officers, directors, managers, presidents, deans, superintendents, bishops, or other officers within institutions. Leadership is defined in terms of supervisory and oversight functions. The office itself is the major source of authority, and the expectations and goals of the institutions determine the selection, equipping, functioning, and tenure of those designated as leaders.

While a popular topic of research and discussion, no consensus exists as to what constitutes leadership. It is often defined by a set of skills or functions directed toward positively influencing institutions. Recruitment and training are then oriented to identifying persons with appropriate personal qualities and organizational skills to move institutions toward developing and achieving quantifiable goals.

Leadership may also be seen as a quality of *being* as much as or more than *doing*. Leadership is a way of being that influences others toward a common vision, mission, and purpose. This is especially true when the goals are identified more in terms of personal or societal values than measurable institutional results.

Attention may also be devoted to defining the qualities of *character* that constitute leadership, rather than the skills required to fulfill functions. The adjectives modifying "leadership" point to the desired values—*moral* leadership, *spiritual* leadership, *compassionate* leadership, *visionary* leadership. Character formation, emotional and relational health, and interpersonal capacities may also be seen as critical components of leadership recruitment and development.

Added to the complexity inherent in defining leadership is the relationship between individual and corporate leadership. If leadership is understood as something one person, designated as *the leader*, executes through particular skills or with distinctive characteristics, then it becomes difficult for a community to practice. Less attention is then given to what it means for institutions, communities, and organizations to exercise corporate leadership. By drawing upon the Christian—and specifically the Wesleyan tradition—a more integrated and textured understanding of leadership may be gained.

Structure of the Book

This book draws upon aspects of the early Methodist movement in Great Britain, led by John Wesley, in order to distill instructive and formative marks of leadership for the church in the world today. The first three chapters identify key components of a frame for Christian leadership inspired by John Wesley and the early Methodist movement: doctrinal foundations, specifically divine grace, and the significance of Christian practices for leadership formation. These chapters engage primary sources from John Wesley, such as sermons and letters, with reflections for faithful and effective leadership practice in the church today. The fourth chapter suggests possibilities for application of themes and material from the earlier chapters to the contemporary context. Each chapter includes a number of features of leadership, distilled from leadership formation in the early Methodist movement that may provide constructive guidance for the informing and shaping of Christian leaders and communities.

Chapter 1 locates the *telos*, or goal, of Christian discipleship and leadership in the mission of the triune God and God's reign. God's reign and mission provide the substance of the doctrinal foundations that frame the church's participation in the transformation of the world. Constitutive to understanding God's mission and reign in the world is salvation in its many dimensions: personal, communal, and cosmic.

Chapter 2 unpacks the significance of divine grace for understanding and practicing leadership in the Wesleyan tradition in light of God's mission to invite all creation to enjoy salvation in Jesus Christ through the Holy Spirit. This chapter explores key experiences and events shaped by divine grace in John Wesley's formation and transformation for leadership.

Chapter 3 explores the central place of Christian practices, or means of grace, for leadership formation in the early Methodist movement. Drawing on insights from John Wesley's sermon "Causes of the Inefficacy of Christianity," the chapter is organized around the integration of doctrine, discipline, and self-denial practiced within community as means of formation in grace. Participating in practices of piety and mercy can facilitate God's work of sanctification in us, encouraging holiness of heart and life for Christian leaders in the world, but not of it.

Chapter 4 describes the contemporary context in which Christian leadership occurs, including the complex and often difficult landscape of competing worldviews in the midst of a disestablished Christian church. In this chapter we acknowledge opportunities and challenges of this landscape, and suggest qualities and skills necessary for embracing its opportunities and confronting its challenges.

The conclusion offers an overview of the marks of Christian leadership drawn from the early Methodist movement as discussed throughout the book for guidance in contemporary practice. Charles Wesley's hymn captured the formative, guiding, and empowering role of divine grace in the work of those who seek to follow and lead as Christian disciples. Read a few of its anointed verses:

Forth in Thy name, O Lord, I go,
my daily labor to pursue;
Thee, only Thee, resolved to know
in all I think or speak or do.

The task Thy wisdom hath assigned,
O let me cheerfully fulfill;
in all my works Thy presence find,
and prove Thy good and perfect will.

Thee may I set at my right hand,
whose eyes mine inmost substance see,
and labor on at Thy command,
and offer all my works to Thee.

For Thee delightfully employ
whate'er Thy bounteous grace hath given;
and run my course with even joy,
and closely walk with Thee to heav'n.[3]

Chapter 1

Christian Leadership Grounded in Doctrine and Mission

W hat is the primary role of a bishop?" a respected theologian and teacher was asked. "Hold the church to theological integrity and discipline," was the response. The wise mentor added that the church's mission is grounded in God—a *particular* God—and that the principal threat to its fulfillment is what John Wesley called "practical atheism" and Parker Palmer has called "functional atheism."[1] Practical atheism assumes the existence of God, but the assumed God has little or no impact on the goals and actions of the believer.

A leader who is a functional or practical atheist believes in God and uses the language of theology but derives vision, motivation, and practices for leading primarily from nontheological sources. Corporate business practices and organizational theory, rather than being subservient tools, become the foundation and primary sources for leadership. The church's doctrine and theology are relegated to the realm of the abstract and the rhetorical. Leadership is thereby motivated, formed, and evaluated anthropologically rather than theologically.

The head of a Fortune 500 company told a group of church leaders, "You are looking to business to teach you about leadership. You should be teaching business leaders. You are the ones who know about real vision, mission, service, and how people are to be treated." It is interesting that leadership scholars are increasingly using the language of theology—vision, mission, presence, hope, community—while many religious leaders are opting for the language of the corporate world: strategy, systems, structures, marketing, processes.

Perhaps the time is right for church leaders and business/institutional leaders to learn from one another without forfeiting the unique contributions of each. Pastors, district superintendents, bishops, boards, and general agency staff members can learn much from the studies and practices of organizational and business scholars and practitioners. They can also provide valuable insights for understanding how systems, organizations, and institutions function most effectively and provide handles for influencing institutional and organizational cultures.

When seen and evaluated through Christian theological lenses, leadership principles espoused by such thinkers as Ron Heifetz and Jim Collins have the potential to deepen our theological foundations and enhance the church's effectiveness in fulfilling its mission. However, without a firm grounding in the church's doctrine and mission, those insights and principles become improved means to unimproved ends; and they become a form of "works righteousness," which adds to the burdens of pastors and church leaders as something else to learn and master in order to be "a good leader."

Many institutions, businesses, and governmental organizations are led by Christian laity who want to incorporate their faith into the practice of leadership. One such leader commented, "My church provides me a strong community and it helps me make personal ethical and moral decisions; but I need more help in connecting my daily responsibilities as a CEO to my faith. How does my business relate to God's mission in the world? Does it have anything to do with the reign of God?"

A president of a church-related college remarked, "When I became president, I went to the Harvard Business School's executive education program to get oriented as to how to manage a complex institution. Where do I go to learn what it means to be the president of a church-related college? How does my leadership of this institution further the mission of the church, and what spiritual practices will help me fulfill the mission?"

Christian leadership, whether in the local church, in church-related institutions, or in secular institutions headed by Christian laity, is grounded in the triune God. Doctrine and theology, therefore, are foundational for understanding and practicing Christian leadership.

The Role of Doctrine, Theology, and Mission in Christian Leadership

There has been a decline in familiarity with the basic stories, doctrines, and affirmations of the Christian faith in the United States. Whereas many stories and passages from the Bible were part of the cultural milieu in earlier American society, one can no longer assume that allusions to biblical images or doctrinal affirmations will be understood by those within the church, much less the general population.

According to scholars, those engaged in the ministries of the church have experienced a waning in theological aptitude. This has resulted in a lack of theological reflection related to Christian practices, including evangelism and leadership. Both John Wesley and Jonathan Edwards were considered great scholars, leaders, and practitioners of Christian faith and ministry in their generations; their influence extended beyond the church into the broader society. However, the beginnings of a major shift may be detected during the nineteenth century, when a growing apathy for the intellectual pursuits and lack of interest in theological discourse in the public arena and within the church's engagement in mission and evangelism occurred.[2]

Science and technology, economics and marketing, politics and government, sociology and psychology, systems and organizational theory dominate the contemporary public discourse and shape personal and institutional practices. Theology has been marginalized as a serious subject or source of relevant knowledge or practice. The salvation narrative of Scripture, Christian doctrine and tradition, and spiritual formation practices have been superseded by the social sciences and business practices as fundamental to leadership formation.

The United Methodist "Doctrinal Standards and Our Theological Task" provides a helpful affirmation of the place of doctrine and theology in the Christian community. *The Book of Discipline* states: "Our doctrinal affirmations assist us in the discernment of Christian truth in ever-changing contexts. Our theological task includes the testing, renewal, elaboration, and application of our doctrinal perspective in carrying out our calling 'to spread scriptural holiness over these lands.'"[3]

It is important to distinguish between doctrine and theological exploration. Doctrine represents the communal formulations of the essential elements or characteristics of the faith. The Articles of Religion and the Confession of Faith, for example, are the formulations of the basic beliefs or affirmations agreed

21

upon by the community. Though the language and imagery must be interpreted, they define the essential categories or concepts of the Christian faith. Doctrines provide the framework and parameters for understanding the faith and exploring its meaning. Theology is the ongoing process of clarifying, interpreting, expanding, and applying the doctrines to Christian belief and practice.

Thomas Langford has suggested a helpful analogy for understanding the place of doctrine and theology in the Christian life. "Doctrine is like a house that a religious community already inhabits. It represents a communal agreement about what is essential to and characteristic of the faith." Theological inquiry "is the proposal of blueprints for extending the house. . . . [T]hese blueprints represent creative efforts to suggest new construction which will make the home more welcoming and adequate."[4]

Christian leadership involves persistent and faithful engagement of doctrine and theology. Christian discipleship and leadership begins, continues, and ends in the God we call the Trinity—Father, Son, and Holy Spirit. Belief in God is widespread in American culture and God's existence is presumed among the church and its leaders, but the particular qualities and purposes of God are undefined and speculative. God becomes an abstract idea rather than a present and ultimate reality that shapes how persons and institutions live and lead.

Christians believe in a *particular* God, whose nature and purposes have been made known and whose qualities, intentions, and activities are the foundation of the church's existence, the source of its power, and the vision of its future. Leadership in the Christian community requires understanding of, commitment to, and relationship with God, who is incarnate in Jesus Christ, witnessed to in Holy Scripture, and present through the Holy Spirit active within community.

Theology—knowledge of, explorations about, love for, and relationship with God—is the substance of Christian leadership. The primary theological questions that occupy Christian leaders are these: Who is God? Where is God? What is God doing? What is God's relationship to the world and our community of faith? What is my relationship with God? Anchored in doctrine, Christian leaders are theologians and teachers. They are persistently identifying, clarifying, and interpreting the nature and purposes of God to and with the people who are called to share in God's mission in the world.

Doctrine and theology, therefore, play the critical role in the formation and practice of Christian leaders. Although United Methodists are often popularly described as people who lack commitment to creedal formulations, doctrine serves essential and primary functions in understanding God and the church's mission, as well as in defining the origin, identity, motivation, and goal of leaders.

Throughout the history of the church, the pastoral task centered in forming a Christian worldview in believers and guiding them in practices and habits that shaped persons and communities in accordance with such a worldview. For Methodists, doctrine serves as a lens through which we view God and the world. Doctrine and theology help form our worldview, the framework for viewing all reality and for orienting our lives. Randy Maddox has described the formational role of doctrine and theology as worldview:

> *A person's worldview is not simply one set of beliefs/disposi-*
> *tions alongside others which he or she embraces; these specific*
> *beliefs/dispositions frame the perspective within which the*
> *person makes sense of, evaluates, and incorporates all other*
> *beliefs and dispositions. That is why the term* theology *should*
> *not be restricted to designating only knowledge of God (as the*
> *Greek roots of the word might imply). It is inadequate even to*
> *confine it to knowledge of general religious truths. It names*
> *instead the Christian practice of approaching all of life from,*
> *and placing all knowledge within, the perspective of God's*
> *revelation in Christ Jesus.*[5]

Methodism did not originate in complex doctrinal disputes or distinctions from other Christian traditions. Instead, a simple, authentic, scriptural Christianity framed the movement. Exposure to doctrine through John Wesley's sermons and treatises, and particularly through Charles's hymns, evangelized and nurtured individuals in the Christian faith and defined the mission of the movement.

For this reason, church leaders, both lay and clergy, considered their primary calling to invite individuals and communities into this worldview, nurture them in practices that formed them accordingly, and prepare them for engagement in the world on behalf of God's revelation in Christ Jesus. As Randy Maddox has affirmed:

> *Their theological energies were necessarily dominated by the*
> *task of forming a Christian worldview in new believers, and*

they pursued this task with a clear sense that the cultures within which they lived were bent on instilling quite different world-views. In this context they prized most highly as "theologians" those who crafted such formative practical-theological materials as hymns, liturgies, catechetical orations, and spiritual discipline manuals.[6]

Leaders in the Wesleyan tradition, then, are grounded in, formed and motivated by, and directed toward a Christian worldview as expressed in Christ Jesus and framed in the church's doctrine and theology. Doctrine and theology are the primary, foundational sources for defining the role and practices of Christian leaders; and all other sources are critiqued in the light of Christian doctrine and theology. Inviting people into the Christian worldview, nurturing them in individual and communal practices that shape them in "the mind of Christ" (1 Cor. 2:16 KJV), and guiding them in engagement in God's mission in the world are the primary functions of pastoral leaders.

Foundational Doctrine and Mission: Holistic Salvation

At the heart of John and Charles Wesley's leadership was a desire "to convince those who would hear what true Christianity was and to persuade them to embrace it." What is "true Christianity," and what are the resources for understanding it? John Wesley named the following as important sources for the early Methodists: "following on *Scripture*; though they generally found, in looking back, something in *Christian antiquity*."[7] These sources would include biblical foundations and the church's practices, or traditions, throughout the centuries since Jesus' ministry. The following four points were "chiefly insisted upon":

First, that orthodoxy, or right opinions, is at best but a very slender part of religion, if it can be allowed to be any part of it at all; that neither does religion consist in negatives, in bare harmlessness of any kind; nor merely in externals, in doing good, or using the means of grace, in works of piety (so called) or of charity: that it is nothing short of or different from the "mind that was in Christ"; the image of God stamped upon the heart; inward righteousness, attended with the peace of God and "joy in the Holy Ghost." . . .

> *Secondly, that the only way under heaven to this religion is to "repent and believe the gospel"; or (as the Apostle words it) "repentance towards God and faith in our Lord Jesus Christ." . . .*

> *Thirdly, that by this faith, "he that worketh not, but believeth on Him that justifieth the ungodly, is justified freely by His grace, through the redemption which is in Jesus Christ." . . .*

> *And, lastly, that "being justified by faith," we taste of the heaven to which we are going, we are holy and happy, we tread down sin and fear, and "sit in heavenly places with Christ Jesus."* [8]

In this way, John, with Charles, emphasized Christian doctrinal foundations of relative simplicity, particularly justification, while hinting at sanctification, from a perspective that resonated with persons' spiritual experiences. At the heart of these doctrinal foundations are concepts such as "the mind of Christ," "image of God," "repentance," "grace," and "taste of heaven."

The comprehensive fundamental doctrine that motivated, framed, and empowered the Methodist movement is what scholars call *soteriology*, or the doctrine of salvation wrought in Jesus Christ. It was their own personal experience of salvation that warmed and transformed their hearts, defined their mission, sent them across the British Isles and beyond, and determined their activities and strategies. Salvation is the theme that ran through John Wesley's preaching, teaching, and writing and Charles Wesley's sermons and hymns. Their experience and understanding of and commitment to holistic salvation resulted in the formation of small groups as communities of support and accountability, and the establishment of schools, medical clinics, lending programs, and cooperatives for the working poor.

The *telos* of Wesleyan and Christian leadership is salvation—of individuals, communities, and the entire creation. Defining salvation, however, has challenged the church throughout the centuries; the concept remains somewhat elusive and abstract for contemporary Christians. John Wesley dealt with the question in his preaching and writing. He raised the question directly in his sermon "The Scripture Way of Salvation":

> *What is salvation? The salvation which here is spoken of is not*

what is frequently understood by that word, the going to heaven, eternal happiness . . . it is a present thing . . . the entire work of God, from the first dawning of grace in the soul till it is consummated in glory. . . . There is a real as well as a relative change. We are inwardly renewed by the power of God. We feel the "love of God shed abroad in our heart by the Holy Ghost which is given unto us," producing love to all humankind.[9]

In a different sermon, he elaborated.

By salvation I mean, not barely (according to the vulgar notion) deliverance from hell, or going to heaven, but a present deliverance from sin, a restoration of the soul to its primitive health, its original purity; a recovery of the divine nature; the renewal of our souls after the image of God in righteousness and true holiness, in justice, mercy, and truth. This implies all holy and heavenly tempers, and by consequences all holiness of conversation.[10]

Salvation is the forgiveness of sinful humanity and the restoration of the divine image, the reconciliation of all things to God, the healing of the whole creation, and the consummation of God's reign of compassion, justice, generosity, and joy in Jesus Christ. Salvation encompasses the individual human heart, motivations, and actions; the complex and intricate fabric of human community; and the mysterious, expansive, and often terrifying natural order.

In the Wesleyan tradition, dialectics, or creative tensions balancing seemingly opposing priorities, are essential to understanding salvation. Salvation includes both God's unmerited gift *and* human initiative and response. It is both a present reality *and* a future expectation; it is already present *and* yet awaits final consummation. Salvation is both instantaneous/immediate *and* also gradual/continuing. It is individual *and* personal, as well as communal *and* social. Clarifying the dialectic and providing resources for living God's salvation are primary responsibilities of pastoral leaders who are faithful to the Wesleyan tradition.

Numerous terms have been used to describe the experience and consequences of salvation in Jesus Christ. John Wesley described this holistic salvation with various images in his sermons, treatises, and other writings: "holiness of heart of life," "love of God shed abroad in our hearts," "having the mind of Christ," "justification," "sanctification," "Christian perfection," "the new creation," or "the kingdom of God."

Integral to leadership is a coherent vision big and comprehensive enough to energize, inspire, and mobilize individuals and communities toward something new. What could be more energizing, inspiring, and mobilizing than the trust in and commitment to God's salvation of the whole creation? Soteriology and eschatology (the study of end times) are central doctrines of the Christian tradition as understood and practiced by "the people called Methodists,"[11] and they are fertile ground for exploring and practicing leadership in the Wesleyan tradition. Understanding vision and mission through the lens of God's present and future salvation pushes the Christian leader beyond the limitations of narrow vision and mission statements in a strategic plan.

Personal Dimensions of Salvation by Grace

The doctrine of salvation permeated John Wesley's life and work, and it constituted the basic framework of the mission of the Methodists. His understanding of salvation was sufficiently comprehensive to provide the overarching vision and motivation for his long and fruitful life and ministry.

At the heart of John Wesley's soteriology is the forgiveness, assurance, and healing wrought in the individual through the saving work of Jesus Christ and experienced through the Holy Spirit. Central to his leadership was his own experience of pardon and assurance. In 1738, he proclaimed: "Christian faith is then not only an assent to the whole gospel of Christ, but also . . . a trust in the merits of his life, death, and resurrection. . . . It is the sure confidence which a [man] hath in God, that through the merits of Christ *his* sins are forgiven, and *he* is reconciled to the favour of God."[12]

He wrote to a friend in 1757, "I hold as divine evidence or conviction that Christ loved *me* and gave Himself for *me* is essential to if not the very essence of justifying faith."[13]

This personal experience of pardon and forgiveness is preceded by what John Wesley called *preventing* or *prevenient grace*. Grace precedes our decision or even our conscious awareness of the presence of and need for forgiveness. Grace prevents the total destruction of the divine image in us and is ever working to woo and prod us toward *justifying grace*, which is forgiveness and pardon and assurance that we are beloved and redeemed sons and daughters of God. But grace does not stop with forgiveness and assurance. *Sanctifying grace* restores the divine image and persistently moves us toward "holiness of heart and life," the love of God shed abroad in our hearts.

While personal forgiveness, pardon, assurance, and holiness were central for John Wesley, personal salvation included more than deliverance from sin and guilt. He often spoke of salvation in the medical language of healing. In a letter to Alexander Knox in 1778, he wrote: "It will be a double blessing if you give yourself up to the Great Physician, that He may heal soul and body together. And unquestionably this is His design. He wants to give you . . . both inward and outward health."[14] The total integration of personality and relationship is the ongoing expression and goal of salvation through grace.

For John Wesley, the key and foremost quality of a leader, especially of clergy, was grace.[15] Does the leader show evidence of forgiveness, reconciliation, and growth in love for God and neighbor? The significance of the personal wholeness of the leader cannot be understated; essential to the Christian leader is the experience of prevenient, justifying, and sanctifying grace.

Social and Communal Dimensions of Salvation by Grace

Salvation through grace extends beyond the forgiveness and reconciliation of individuals to themselves and to God. God's healing, reconciling, and transforming presence and power extend to society and the social structures and dimensions of human existence. Grace is more than a reality in the inner lives of individuals; it is present as the power of healing and reconciliation in relationships. An oft-quoted Methodist affirmation is: "The gospel of Christ knows no religion, but social; no holiness but social holiness."[16]

A fuller description of the social dimensions of salvation through grace is found in John Wesley's preaching:

> *Christianity is essentially a social religion. . . . [T]o turn it into a solitary religion, is indeed to destroy it. . . . I mean not only that it cannot subsist so well, but that it cannot subsist at all, without society—without living and conversing with other [people]. . . . That religion described by our Lord cannot subsist without society*

> *. . . is manifest from hence, that several of the most essential*
> *branches thereof can have no place if we have no intercourse with*
> *the world. There is no disposition, for instance, which is more*
> *essential to Christianity than meekness. . . . Another necessary*
> *branch of true Christianity is peace-making, or doing good.*[17]

For John Wesley, the essence of salvation is love for God and neighbor; and such love is expressed in doing good to all persons, "unto neighbors, and strangers, friends, and enemies. And that in every possible kind; not only to their bodies, by 'feeding the hungry, clothing the naked, visiting those that are sick or in prison,' but much more does he labour to do good to their souls."[18]

Grace is a relational reality and can only be nurtured in communities of support and accountability. Salvation cannot be hoarded as a private possession of the pious; it must flow generously to others in acts of compassion, mercy, and justice. As God's grace overflows in the creation of the world and fashioning of human beings in the divine image, in redeeming and reconciling fallen humanity, and supremely in the life, death, and resurrection of Jesus Christ, so that grace must spill over through us to the wounded, hurting, alienated, and broken places in the human family.

Such a sense of the lavish and extravagant grace of God propelled John Wesley to the margins of eighteenth-century England and motivated him to invest a lifetime in ministry with the poor, the imprisoned, the sick, and the underresourced people of his day. He challenged the social forces that threatened the well-being and wholeness of persons, such as the slave trade, unfair lending practices, the liquor traffic, and child labor. He provided personal aid and established institutions for the advancement of well-being of persons left out of the mainstream of society. Such leadership was the consequence of a vision of God's grace working to heal, reconcile, and transform the human family in accordance with God's present and coming reign in Jesus Christ.

Cosmic Dimensions of Salvation by Grace

Since God's presence and power, or grace, extends to the far reaches of the universe, God's salvation reaches beyond human hearts and communities. The psalmist declares, "Your steadfast love, O LORD, extends to the heavens, your faithfulness to the clouds. Your righteousness is like the mighty mountains, your judgments are like the great deep; you save humans and animals alike, O LORD" (Ps. 36:5–6).

Paul proclaims that the salvation wrought in Jesus Christ has brought into being a whole new creation (2 Cor. 5). Through Christ, God "was pleased to reconcile to himself all things, whether on earth or in heaven, by making peace through the blood of his cross" (Col. 1:20). God's grace incarnate in Jesus Christ has redeemed and is transforming the whole creation.

While creation awaits the final consummation of the salvation brought near in Jesus Christ, grace incarnate, the vision of the new heaven and the new earth motivates and empowers the church's ongoing mission to be a sign and instrument of God's cosmic salvation. Such a vision pervades John Wesley's leadership and preaching, especially in his later years.

He described the eschatological vision of a new creation this way:

> All the elements . . . will be new[,] indeed entirely changed as to their qualities, although not as to their nature. . . . All the earth shall then be a more beautiful paradise than Adam ever saw. . . . He that sitteth upon the throne will soon change the face of all things, and give demonstrative proof to all his creatures that "his mercy is over all his works." The horrid state of things which at present obtains, will soon be at an end. On earth, no creature will kill, or hurt, or give pain to any other. The scorpion will have no poisonous sting; the adder, no venomous teeth. The lion will have no claws to tear the lamb; no teeth to grind his flesh and bones. Nay, no creature, no beast, bird, or fish, will have any inclination to hurt any other; for cruelty will be far away, and savageness and fierceness be forgotten. So that violence shall be heard no more, neither wasting or destruction seen on the face of the earth. "The wolf shall dwell with the lamb," (the words may be literally as well as figuratively understood) "and the leopard shall lie down with the kid. They shall not hurt or destroy, 'from the rising up of the sun, to the going down of the same.'"[19]

John Wesley added in the same sermon that even the blazing, falling stars would be transformed, and order and harmony will govern the stars and planets.

God's grace abounds throughout the created order. God's grace through the Holy Spirit is ever active to create, heal, reconcile, and transform everything in accordance with the reign of God incarnate in Jesus Christ. That is the fundamental, bedrock doctrine that calls forth, forms, sustains, empowers, and guides leaders who are faithful to the Wesleyan tradition.

Who is God? God is the Father who creates the world through grace, the Son who redeems the world through grace, and the Holy Spirit who transforms the world through grace.

Where is God? God's presence permeates the entire creation, from the minute microscopic cell to the yet undiscovered planet in an undetected galaxy in the infinite reaches of space.

What is God doing? God is bringing salvation. God's grace is creating, healing, forgiving, reconciling, and transforming

- human hearts and lives;
- human communities and societies;
- the earth's forces, creatures, and institutions; and
- the mysterious celestial worlds of an infinite universe.

What is the appropriate response to the triune God who is bringing salvation? We are invited and called to share in God's salvation by being formed and transformed by grace and by participating in the *missio Dei*. As participants in God's mission, we are called to nurture individuals and communities that are visible signs, foretastes, and instruments of God's salvation.

Leaders as Theologians

Metaphors matter when it comes to shaping persons and communities. The Bible contains scores of metaphors for those called to share in God's mission of salvation. "People of God," "holy nation," God's "flock," "body of Christ," "household of God," "new creation," and "fellowship of faith" are only a few of the descriptive images of the church. Those images, however, shape how congregations see themselves and their mission.

Metaphors matter when it comes to shaping the identity and functions of those who are set apart to lead congregations and institutions. What is the compelling metaphor of Christian leaders, especially pastors? Among the most historically prominent are *shepherd, pastor, priest, prophet, minister, teacher, evangelist,* and *preacher.* Only in recent years has the term *leader* emerged as a prominent metaphor to describe the persons who have been called and set apart to share in advancing God's mission through the church. The current emphasis on leaders and leadership is significantly influencing the identity and function of pastors and others who are set apart for the church's mission and ministry.

Leaders tend to be identified primarily with institutions and organizations. Leaders are commonly understood as those who foster the growth, efficiency, and expansion of institutions and organizations. When the advancement of institutions becomes the primary *telos* of leadership, the foundational resources for the development of leaders are organizational theory and management principles and techniques. Strategic planning, marketing, personnel motivation, and development become principal tools and methods.

In the Christian community, something supersedes the institution as the anchor and focus of leaders. Pervading the life and action of those called to share in God's mission of salvation is devotion to and relationship with the triune God. A Christian leader is first and always a follower of Jesus Christ, a disciple. Christian leadership, then, is paradoxically derivative of Christian discipleship.

Without a consistent and firm anchor in theology, the pursuit of leadership can be seductive and counterproductive in the same way that striving to be humble can produce arrogance and phoniness. And it can result in the cultivation of skills in manipulation and coercion directed toward undesirable personal and institutional goals.

Resident theologian has occasionally been used as descriptive of the primary role of the one who leads local congregations; however, few clergy consciously consider themselves theologians. Theologians are more popularly considered to be the professional, academic scholars and teachers of theology. Nevertheless, theology is at the heart of the identity and function of those persons devoted to sharing in God's mission of salvation and shaping communities that reflect God's mission.

Christian doctrine and theology form the identity, motivation, vision, and practices of those called to participate as leaders in God's mission of salvation of the cosmos. The Christian leader views the world through the lens of who God is, where God is, what God is doing, and what God invites and calls us to. For the Christian leader, all issues have theological components, all experiences contain potential avenues of God's presence, all relationships include opportunities to embody Christ's loving presence, and all challenges represent possible pathways to advancing God's salvation.

Since God's presence and power to create, heal, redeem, reconcile, and transform the whole creation are pervasive and unceasing, the Christian leader is ever discerning where and how the divine presence and power are manifest and where God is leading the way forward. The Christian leader's vocation is derived from and formed and empowered by the *missio Dei*. The redemption, reconciliation, healing, and transformation of human hearts and minds, community structures and relationships, and the entire created order are the overarching goal of the Christian leader.

The theologically formed leader distinguishes between the ultimate and the penultimate. The reign of God made known in Jesus Christ is the ultimate *telos* of history; and the bringing near of the consummation of God's reign of compassion, justice, generosity, peace, joy, and hope is the goal of all ministry.

The church is the penultimate goal of the Christian leader. The church exists as sign, herald, foretaste, and instrument of the Ultimate—the reign of God over all creation. Therefore, the criterion by which the church leader is evaluated is how closely the institution resembles and practices God's reign and how faithfully it shares in God's mission of creating, healing, forgiving, redeeming, reconciling, and transforming persons, communities, and creation.

Leaders, therefore, are resident theologians. Their identity, worldview, and vocation are anchored in, formed and empowered by, and directed toward God's salvation through grace. They live and move and have their being in theology—God's revelation, presence, and mission. As theologians they discern and interpret who God is, where God is, what God is doing, and what our relationship is to the nature and presence and mission of God.

Leadership in the Wesleyan tradition requires deep and broad knowledge of Scripture and the Christian tradition, as well as the intersection of Scripture and tradition with contemporary contexts. But more than knowledge is required. Grace-formed character that embodies the truth of Scripture and tradition characterizes those who are called to share in God's mission. Leaders also have skills in forming and nurturing communities that embody the truth of Scripture and tradition and are visible signs, foretastes, and instruments of God's new creation.

Marks of Christian Leadership Formed by Doctrine, Theology, and Mission

What qualities characterize leaders who are grounded in and formed by Christian doctrine and theology?

Practicing leadership in the Wesleyan tradition involves an understanding of and formation in Scripture and the Christian tradition with the ability to appropriate the gospel in contemporary contexts. Central to the leadership of John and Charles Wesley was a deep understanding of and formation in basic Christian doctrine as revealed in Scripture and the church's tradition. Perhaps no one in the eighteenth century was more familiar with Scripture and the doctrines and practices of the early church than John Wesley; and no one was more intent on forming people and communities in those doctrines and traditions.

Contemporary Wesleyan leaders interpret reality through the presence, purposes, promises, and revelations of the triune God. The images, language, and affirmations of the Bible, doctrine, and theology form the mind-set of the leader and the basic framework by which all life is experienced and interpreted. The character of the leader is formed by practices and experiences that cultivate "the mind of Christ," "the *imago Dei*," "holiness of heart and life," and "the entire love of God shed abroad in our hearts."

Theological reflection is an essential component of leadership practiced in the Wesleyan tradition. John Wesley was obsessed with knowing God, living the reign of God, and proclaiming and teaching the truth of God made known in Jesus Christ and through the Holy Spirit. His sermons and other writings were theological through and through. Theological reflection was no occasional diversion from pastoral, administrative, or evangelistic duties. It was the thread that held together the fabric of his ministry, and he expected no less of his preachers, class leaders, and stewards.

Faithful leadership in the Wesleyan tradition sees the theological components of all experiences, issues, and challenges. Theology becomes the integrating factor of all knowledge and experience. Such leaders persistently ask the questions, Who is God? Where is God present? What is God doing? What is God's mission/purpose? What does God desire for us and the world? Such theological reflection is appropriately done in community with others who are seeking to know God and to fulfill the divine mission.

Leadership formed by doctrine, theology, and mission places priority on teaching and formation. "Practical divinity" characterizes Wesleyan theology and practice. John and Charles Wesley devoted themselves to imparting the Christian faith to the people of eighteenth-century England through sermons, essays, treatises, letters, hymns, and liturgy. They were not academic or systematic theologians, and yet they were theologians and teachers of the first order. The goal of their teaching, however, was more than the transmission of information. They were occupied with the formation of persons and communities in accordance with the doctrines and practices of the Christian faith. Theirs was a lived theology expressed in inviting persons into God's salvation, forming them as disciples or what John Wesley called "real Christians," and engaging them in mission in the world.

A dominant image of a leader today is that of manager of an institution. Strategic planning, personnel and fiscal management, and administrative supervision receive priority attention by those designated as leaders. Pastors increasingly feel pulled by the demands of running a complex organization; and their effectiveness is measured by the efficiency and statistical strength of the organization.

But many in the leadership education field now talk about the necessity of being "a learning organization," with the primary task of the leader to facilitate learning by that organization. Leaders who know John Wesley see themselves as teachers, facilitators of learning and formation. Every situation and circumstance is seen as a teaching opportunity, a context for identifying who God is, where God is, what God is doing, and what God expects of us.

Leaders in the Wesleyan tradition have a passionate sense of vocational calling to share in the missio Dei. From his childhood, when he was rescued from the burning manse at Epworth at the age of five, John Wesley felt that God had a claim on his life. Following that frightening and potentially catastrophic event, his mother, Susanna, considered him to be "a brand plucked from the burning," spared by divine providence for a purpose. With his father as an Anglican priest and role model and his mother as a spiritual guide, John Wesley pursued the general calling to holy living and the specific calling to holy orders. Sharing in God's salvation was the passion of his life. It shaped his education, his sojourn in America, his spiritual disciplines and practices, and his leadership of the renewal movement.

The recent writings on leadership identify such virtues as passion, commitment, courage, and perseverance as integral to strong leaders. Though such scholars seldom use the language of calling, the concept is widely recognized as essential. The conviction that our life and work have transcendent meaning and purpose characterizes those who practice leadership in the Wesleyan tradition. God has called us to share in God's mission of the salvation of the world. We are part of a much larger vocation than promoting self-interest or narrow institutional agendas.

Leadership formed by the Wesleyan doctrine of holistic salvation is characterized by hope. John Wesley's confidence in God's ultimate victory over sin and death and his faith in the consummation of the reign of God brought near in Jesus Christ account for his perseverance and hope in the face of obstacles and challenges. For him, the decisive victory over the principalities and powers that thwart God's salvation was won in the life, death, and resurrection of Jesus Christ. Therefore, current sufferings and defeats are temporary. They can be confronted and endured in the assurance that God's salvation will be brought to completion.

Scholars of leadership document that hope is an essential component of effective leaders of organizations. One such scholar has written, "High hope individuals are better able to cope with ambiguity and uncertainty and, indeed, are energized by the challenge of journeying into an undefined future without having all the answers yet knowing that in time the answers will be revealed." He added: "When people hope, their stance is not only that reality is open, but also that it is continually becoming."[20] In most leadership resources "hope" is an expression of positivistic psychology. Hope in Wesleyan theology, on the other hand, is grounded in eschatology, God's consummation of the salvation wrought in Jesus Christ. Therefore, leaders formed by Wesleyan doctrine and mission exhibit hope grounded in what God has done, is doing, and will do.

Leadership formed by doctrine, theology, and mission is characterized by an audacious, comprehensive vision that transcends but includes the institutional church. Methodism began as a renewal movement within the Church of England. John Wesley's efforts transcended growth in mere numbers of adherents to the Church of England. John Wesley was convinced that God had raised up Methodists "to reform the nation and, in particular the Church, and to spread scriptural holiness over the land." The salvation of human hearts, communities, nations, and the entire creation was the overarching vision that inspired and shaped the Wesleyan revival. Bringing the vision of a healed and transformed creation into reality was the mission of the early Methodists.

All effective leadership requires a compelling vision that motivates change toward a new future. The vision must be comprehensive and audacious enough to inspire and yet realistic enough to be at least partially attainable. At the heart of the Christian gospel as expressed in doctrine is a vision of a new creation redeemed and transformed in Jesus Christ. Leaders in the Wesleyan tradition keep that vision in the forefront and evaluate everything in the light of that vision. They place the mission of the church in that broader vision, which enables them to avoid limiting vision of leadership to statistical growth. They seek to lead the church to incorporate and approximate this transcendent vision, and they measure their leadership by how closely the church resembles and furthers God's vision of a redeemed and transformed creation.

Conclusion

Christian leadership as understood and practiced in the Wesleyan tradition is first and foremost about God, the God we know as Trinity—Father, Son, and Holy Spirit. The doctrines of the Christian faith represent formulations and descriptions of the triune God agreed upon by the church. Doctrine serves as the lens through which we view the world and the church's life and mission. Theology is the ongoing interpretation and appropriation of the doctrine in light of current realities, opportunities, and challenges.

Central to doctrine as understood and practiced in the Wesleyan tradition is God's salvation of the world. All leadership, therefore, emerges from and is directed toward the *missio Dei*—God's mission of the redemption and transformation of human hearts, communities, nations, and the entire cosmos. Christian leaders are formed by God's salvation and they are devoted to sharing in God's mission through their vocation as baptized Christians, as those called and set apart to nurture persons and institutions in accordance with the Christian gospel.

Leadership can be a heavy burden upon sincere and dedicated people. However, leadership as understood and practiced in the Wesleyan tradition is a gift to be identified, nurtured, celebrated, and deployed as a participation in God's salvation. Fundamental to salvation is God's initiative and action on behalf of creation. That divine action and all Wesleyan leadership are birthed, called forth, nurtured, and empowered by *grace*. We now turn to a fuller consideration of leadership formed and transformed by grace.

Questions for Reflection and Discussion

1. Why did John and Charles Wesley put forth so much effort to provide Methodist leaders with resources about Christian theology and doctrine? Do you believe this is a responsibility for today's Christian leaders? If so, how adequately do you think it is being fulfilled?

2. Describe the different dimensions of salvation by grace. What is lost when the Christian community focuses on only one of these dimensions? Why do leaders need a thorough understanding of all dimensions of salvation?

3. How does the leader's relationship with the triune God shape the leader's exercise of leadership and relationship with the Christian community?

4. What are some competing images of *leader*? What image best describes your leadership style? Which images follow the Christian vision of following the triune God?

Chapter 2

Leadership Formed by Grace

L eadership formation is an essential responsibility of the life of institutions, including the church. Identifying potential leaders, nurturing their capacity and skills, and deploying them in appropriate contexts are crucial to the viability and success of organizations, businesses, agencies, and corporations. The recent emergence of the leadership culture with its guilds, institutes, consultants, coaches, and expanding literature is largely a response to the recognized need for quality leadership formation.

Much leadership formation is directed toward understanding how organizations and systems function, identifying characteristics of leaders, cultivating skills, strategic planning and implementation processes, and deploying and managing personnel for maximum effectiveness. Important lessons can be learned from these efforts, especially in transforming organizations and institutions.

Also important are leadership formation approaches that focus primarily on the personhood of the leaders.[1] These approaches look at the character, values, and personal qualities of those identified as leaders; and they approach leadership development as personality and character formation. The focus is on the temperament, intellect, and relational qualities of leaders. These approaches have close kinship with the spiritual-formation dimensions of leadership formation, which focus on spiritual disciplines and guides as critical tools in the development and sustaining of leaders.

At the heart of the Wesleyan movement of the eighteenth century was John Wesley's own leadership formation, which later informed his intentional cultivation of others, including youth and women for leadership in such roles as class leader, steward, and local preacher. Firm grounding in sound doctrine and theology framed John Wesley's own leadership formation, as well as his development of other leaders in the early Methodist movement.

As we have discussed, *the fundamental and determinative doctrine that shapes the Wesleyan tradition and its leaders is salvation by grace*. John Wesley's holistic vision of salvation and mission was grounded in his understanding of grace offered by God and experienced personally, as well as offered to others, including the poor and those on the margins of English society.

The section that follows surveys John Wesley's early formation that informed his leadership in light of the major themes identified among the marks of leadership in Chapter 1: doctrinal foundations, vocation, and hopeful vision. The remaining sections offer, respectively, a fuller explanation of grace in the Wesleyan tradition and identification of additional marks of leadership drawn from John Wesley's leadership formation.

John Wesley: Formed and Transformed for Leadership

John Wesley led and inspired an international Christian renewal movement. An unlikely leader, Wesley was neither a charismatic nor a commanding figure. For example, George Whitefield was widely known as a more magnetic preacher; and Charles, John's younger brother, consistently demonstrated more tact and skill in nurturing relationships, particularly among the affluent. However, John Wesley's desire for salvation and Christian faithfulness led him to respond not only to contextual dynamics but also to God's grace extended to all in Jesus Christ through the Holy Spirit.

His early formation in faith, both intensely structured and theological, provided a frame within which John Wesley would practice leadership. This leadership was motivated, formed, and characterized by grace that unfolded into a hopeful vision to participate in God's reign and spread scriptural holiness. John Wesley's early formation contributed to this hopeful vision of God's power and presence to redeem and transform human hearts, societies, and the entire creation.

Doctrinal Foundations

Central to John Wesley's leadership formation and vocation within the early Methodist movement were doctrinal foundations, particularly his experience and understanding of grace, which was formed and informed by the influences of family, education, and ministry contexts as a young adult.

John Wesley's family life in childhood was highly structured. John's mother, Susanna Wesley, took very seriously her responsibility to form her children in the Christian faith alongside their father and parish priest, Samuel. John Wesley's education at home and in formal settings, beginning at an early age and stretching through graduate work at Oxford, focused primarily upon theological formation and study toward the discernment of vocation.

Samuel and Susanna Wesley were members of the Church of England but from nonconformist backgrounds. Susanna's father, Samuel Annesley, was a noted nonconformist minister in London in the late seventeenth century.[2] Samuel's father, John Wesley, had been excluded from his ministry by the bishop of Bristol in the 1660s under charges that he was a dissenter disagreeing with the Act of Uniformity, with later implications under the Act of Toleration 1689.[3] Both Samuel and Susanna became "converts" to the established church as young adults.

Samuel and Susanna Wesley worked together to raise their children. John Wesley, or "Jacky," was born on June 17, 1703, the thirteenth or fourteenth child of Samuel and Susanna (Samuel did not keep accurate records of the children his wife birthed—as many as seventeen or eighteen births total). John was the seventh child to survive beyond one year.[4]

Susanna instituted a weekly evening hour with each of the five or six children living in the home at any given time, and her intellect and firm discipline provided a stimulating environment for the children. John, as a child in the Epworth rectory, was the only boy at home with four or five sisters until he was four, when Charles was born. Susanna was ahead of her time in her practice of teaching the girls, as well as the boys to read. Susanna enforced the understanding that "no girl be taught to work till she can read very well since the putting children to learn sewing before they can read perfectly is the very reason why so few women can read fit to be heard, and never to be understood."[5] Theological themes and issues pervaded the correspondence between Susanna and her children, which is surprising for a time in which women largely did not have access to formal education. In this way, John's imagination was opened to include the leadership roles and contributions of women.

Samuel's role as parish priest, together with Susanna's influence, also contributed to an ordered life that included prayers, worship, and study. In addition to the daily and weekly rhythms of worship and prayer, Samuel attempted to organize a small religious society in 1700 at Epworth based on the London model. Resources were ordered from the Society for the Promotion of Christian Knowledge, and Samuel became a corresponding member. Within two years Samuel had established a small society with a set of rules.[6] John Wesley would follow this pattern at Oxford decades later.

Vocational Discernment

Despite, or perhaps because of, John Wesley's seriousness with regard to his spiritual and theological formation, he reluctantly sought ordination in the Church of England. However, as he assumed roles of pastoral leadership, he continued to reflect upon his own questions and experiences of faith that informed his understanding of grace and vocation, as well as ultimately his hopeful and visionary leadership of the early Methodist movement.

John Wesley did not inquire into issues of faith and salvation for only himself. Though Wesley desired his own salvation, he also desired the salvation of others. In this way his leadership, informed by his understanding and experiences of grace, invited others to claim their vocations for Christian leadership within the organization of the early Methodist movement.

Richard Heitzenrater, the leading scholar on John Wesley and early Methodism, states that Wesley's reading in 1725 at Oxford turned to pietism and practices of holy living. The late medieval mystic Thomas à Kempis's *The Imitation of Christ* provided the foundation for Wesley, who then went on to read Jeremy Taylor's *The Rule and Exercises of Holy Living* (1650) and *The Rule and Exercises of Holy Dying* (1651), Robert Nelson's *The Practice of True Devotion* (1698), and William Beveridge's *Private Thoughts upon Religion* (1709). According to Heitzenrater, "Jeremy Taylor provided one of the most crucial suggestions that Wesley adopted: the first rule of holy living is care of your time." The most visible demonstration of Taylor's influence was John Wesley's beginning to keep a diary in subsequent years as a record and measure of his progress in holy living.[7]

According to Heitzenrater, "[T]he most significant theological consequence of the pietist influence was John Wesley's discovery that holiness was an inner reality—'that true religion was seated in the heart and that God's law extended to all our thoughts as well as our words and actions.'" This perspective displays many of the characteristics that came to be called "Methodist."[8] Thus, the personal and communal practices of the emerging "Methodists" grew from John Wesley's desire for Christian faith through holiness of heart and life, which included self-awareness, and clarity of vocation in response to his own doubts.

The influence of John Wesley's parents can be seen in his ongoing vocational discernment as a young person. Discerning a vocation to the scholarly life, he contemplated ordination, a prerequisite for such a path. However, John Wesley faced substantial doubts regarding the appropriateness of his seeking ordination, and thus sought the advice of his parents, which in turn led to his growing self-awareness and commitment to a more disciplined life, and eventually to the rise of Methodism. John Wesley's father encouraged him by saying that there was no harm in his son's motive for entering into holy orders, but added that "a desire and intention to lead a stricter life" was a better reason. His mother concurred, pleased by the "alteration of [his] temper," and sent him a few lines of advice in February 1725: "Dear Jacky, I heartily wish you would now enter upon a serious examination of yourself, that you may know whether you have a reasonable hope of salvation."[9]

Upon his father's death, John Wesley served the Epworth parish for a brief time and then returned to Oxford. Although his place seemed to be in Oxford, an opportunity arose in 1736 to travel to Georgia; and it would be this missionary work to Oglethorpe's Georgia colony that would give John Wesley an opportunity to fulfill his ordination and his father's expectations, as well as to engage in ministry that crossed the boundaries of class and race.

Charles, with a number of others, was recruited to accompany John on this venture. John wrote that he hoped to save his own soul with the hope also of doing good in America. He hoped to learn the true sense of the gospel of Christ through his ministry to those "unspoiled gentiles" and thus be able to attain a higher degree of holiness himself.[10]

A winter crossing in the eighteenth century was not an easy endeavor or without significant risk. Sailing on the *Simmonds*, John Wesley was deeply moved by the powerful storms and threat of death. The question of his salvation had new urgency, and his lack of assurance was apparent. He felt that his fear of death demonstrated his lack of faith. During the third and worst storm, while many of the English passengers screamed with fright, the German Moravians on board calmly continued to sing the psalms without intermission, and Wesley was moved by the depth of their faith.[11]

John Wesley's pastoral experience in Georgia included encountering colonists from England, Native Americans, and enslaved Africans. His first contact with Native Americans on board the *Simmonds* quickly deflated his hope that Native Americans would have no preconceived notions of Christianity. However, there was interest expressed by the Creek chief, who warned John Wesley that the French, Spanish, and English traders had caused great confusion and suspicion. On the other hand, he had a good experience teaching and catechizing enslaved African Americans—a bold move—and he would go on to persistently oppose inhuman treatment, especially slavery.[12]

John Wesley's time in Georgia would not last long. Early on, he had criticized some settlers' attempts to have private baptisms and to omit publishing the marriage bans. Like many young clergy, John Wesley was at times a strict and even intransigent pastor—perhaps even naive and idealistic.

According to Heitzenrater, "Sophey Hopkey's hasty marriage to William Williamson was also personally devastating to Wesley as a suitor, but was also ecclesiastically improper in the eyes of Wesley, the parish priest." He subsequently barred her from Communion, a public affront which led to charges being brought to the grand jury of Savannah against Wesley—charges that claimed he had deviated from the principles of the Established Church. Such charges could have provided the basis for a trial, but John Wesley swiftly and quietly departed the colony before the matter came to court.[13]

John Wesley's vocational journey to this point was hardly smooth. He faced doubts and reluctance to pursue ordination. William Morgan, a fellow Oxford student and "Methodist," whom he followed into the prisons and among the poor, fell ill and died at a young age. Traveling abroad to Georgia challenged John Wesley's idealism regarding ministry with Native Americans, as well as colonists of a similar culture, and ultimately confronted him with the prospect of failure.

However, through these situations and following his return from Georgia, Wesley persistently discerned and followed God's call, looking to mentors, fellow Christians, and books from scholars of another time for clarity and guidance. His willingness to receive God's grace and vocation through these vessels contributed important facets to his self-awareness, openness to ministry, and a hopeful vision for the early Methodist movement.

A significant and traumatic event during John Wesley's childhood—the burning of the rectory and the safe deliverance of all the Wesley children— contributed to a later narration of his unfolding vocation, a narration that emphasized the providential nature of the rescue. By 1737, Wesley had adopted for himself the phrase from the Old Testament prophets, "a brand plucked out of the burning" (Amos 4:11 ESV; see also Zechariah 3:2), which, according to many, indicated not only Wesley's providential deliverance from the fire but also a divine designation of some extraordinary destiny.[14] John Wesley responded to this claim with some humility, but the sense of a divine claim upon his life was real from this early age.[15]

The unfolding sense of vocation was a lifelong process for John Wesley. From his childhood nurture in the Epworth manse and the conviction of being a "brand plucked from the burning" to the pursuit of knowledge and vital piety at Oxford and sojourn in Georgia, Wesley's driving motivation was participation in God's mission of salvation. He remained open to the guidance of the Holy Spirit as he drew insight from others, the Scriptures, the writings and resources from the broad tradition of the church, and his own engagement in works of piety and mercy. His emerging clarity and confidence in his vocational discernment reflected his theological convictions that faith increases as it is exercised, and each act of faithfulness to God's grace and mission opens new avenues of participation in God's grace and mission. Wesley's life, therefore, is a narrative of unfolding clarity and confidence in vocational commitment.

Hopeful Vision

Within a week of John Wesley's return from Georgia, he met Peter Böhler, a Lutheran minister newly arrived from Germany on his way to America. Böhler would influence John Wesley with models for personal piety and renewal, as well as corporate organizational development contributing to his emerging leadership of Methodism.[16]

Böhler pushed John Wesley theologically, insisting that Wesley's lack of personal assurance of salvation indicated a lack of faith, since, in Böhler's view, there are no degrees of faith. As a result, Wesley felt that he could not continue preaching. Böhler responded to John Wesley's predicament with these oft-quoted words: "Preach faith til you have it, and then, because you have it, you will preach faith."[17] Thus, Böhler encouraged John Wesley to live into a hopeful vision, both personally and for the Methodist renewal movement.

Wesley told Böhler of meetings consisting of approximately seventy persons who met for prayer, singing, and Bible study, but which apparently had little organization or supervision. On May 1, 1738, Böhler intervened, composing a set of simple rules. These rules provided the original framework for the Fetter Lane Society, whose organization John Wesley would later call "the third rise of Methodism." When Böhler left three days later for the New World, John Wesley was leader of this nascent movement.[18]

Within days of Böhler's departure, Charles and others became convinced of the Moravian theological perspective that faith converts at once. Charles even experienced an assurance of faith while sick in bed on Whitsunday (Pentecost). He felt "a strange palpitation of heart" and was able to say "I believe, I believe!" finding himself at peace with God. This surprising news put John Wesley into a state of "continual sorrow" until his own experience of assurance that followed his brother's after three long days, on May 24, 1738.[19] He records the events from the Scripture reading in the morning to the anthem at St. Paul's in the afternoon and the society meeting later that day:

> In the evening I went very unwillingly to a society in Aldersgate Street, where one was reading Luther's preface to the epistle to the Romans. About a quarter before nine, while he was describing the change which God works in the heart through faith in Christ, I felt my heart strangely warmed. I felt I did trust in Christ, Christ alone for salvation, and an assurance was given me that he had taken away my sins, even mine, and saved me from the law of sin and death.[20]

He testified to the group of his experience and celebrated with Charles afterward. The teaching of his Moravian mentors now became a confession that he could claim for himself—*Christus pro me*. John Wesley felt that now he was truly a Christian, although several friends doubted John Wesley's claim not to be a Christian until May 24. But the real test of authenticity would not be the warmth of heart but fruits of faith, as the Moravians taught—freedom from sin, doubt, and fear, and the fullness of peace, love, and joy in the Holy Spirit.[21] Alas, there would be doubts and much farther to travel on his theological and spiritual journey, but John Wesley's life was now framed by a new hope and experience of grace.

Following Böhler's admonition to preach faith until he has it and then preach it because he has it, John Wesley reported that the first person to whom he preached "this new doctrine" was a convicted felon, Clifford, with whom he continued the practice of prison visitation.[22] A short year later, John Wesley would reluctantly accept George Whitefield's invitation to engage in "field preaching" among Bristol's coal miners and subsequently thousands of England's working poor.[23] John Wesley's ministry and leadership would maintain a consistent pattern of relationships and practices among the poor throughout his long life.

In Chapter 3, we will explore further the attraction of thousands through field preaching, complemented by an intentional organizational structure of small groups for continued nurture and accountability of growth in grace, which created a vital infrastructure for the hopeful vision and mission of the early Methodist movement.

Growth in Understanding and Experience of Grace

John Wesley is not known as a systematic theologian. Widely read and tirelessly curious, Wesley followed the intellectual currents of his time and context. Significant to understanding John Wesley's theological emphases, one must step back from the intellectual conversations of the time and view these through the lens of Wesley's spiritual journey, as well as those with whom he interacted. While John Wesley was a learned scholar, the questions that most deeply shaped his life and work were questions of faith—theological questions.

As we have seen from John Wesley's formation, he was influenced both by Anglican emphases upon tradition and good works, as well as pietist emphases upon personal experience and assurance. At this intersection, the concept and experience of grace most profoundly grounded John Wesley's life and ministry. For Wesley, located within an Anglo-Catholic tradition, works of both piety and mercy were essential to a Christian life of faith. Operational within this construct and demonstrated across the centuries is an experiential theme—the role of God's multifaceted grace for humankind.

47

John Wesley's understanding of grace among the Christian doctrines and his experiences, which constitute an individual's receiving salvation from God in Jesus Christ through the Holy Spirit, matured throughout his life and ministry. Initially, as demonstrated by his Aldersgate account, the Moravian influence and emphasis upon no degrees of faith was strong. During this period, John Wesley understood with Böhler that good works or fruit meet for repentance could only occur following justification as an aspect of sanctification. So, any good work performed prior to one's justification (repentance of sins and assurance of faith) could not serve God, only self. However, later in his life and ministry, John Wesley came to a more nuanced and complex understanding of grace. This more mature understanding is most clearly demonstrated in Wesley's sermon "Scripture Way of Salvation" (1765). Here, among other sources, Wesley describes the multiple functions of God's grace, put simply as preventing, justifying, and sanctifying grace.

As we emphasized in Chapter 1, grace, for John Wesley, is God's presence and power to save and transform persons, societies, and the whole of creation. Rather than something God dispenses as a commodity, grace *is God* present to create, save, heal, forgive, and transform. As Randy Maddox reminds us, John Wesley combined the Eastern and Western emphases on grace. The Eastern tradition placed the emphasis on grace as healing, and Wesley often used medical images to describe the work of grace. But he also accented grace as forgiveness, which is the dominant emphasis in the Western tradition.[24] Grace, then, is God's presence and power to forgive, reconcile, heal, and transform.

John Wesley often expressed the work of grace as *preventing* (prevenient), *justifying*, and *sanctifying*. Prevenient grace is the grace that goes before, preceding human effort or response, and prevents the total destruction of the divine image in persons. Grace always precedes human awareness, effort, and response; and grace meets us in creation, other people, and every context. Wesley, therefore, proclaimed the gospel with confidence that God was already preparing the hearers to respond. He went into the prisons, the hovels of the poor, and the open fields with courage because he assumed that God's presence and power preceded him; and he was able to launch new initiatives with the assurance that grace would bring to harvest seeds of faithfulness.

Justifying grace assures us that our sins are forgiven, that God has claimed us as beloved sons and daughters, and that God has acted decisively in Jesus

Christ to salvage and restore the divine image in us. Justifying grace, with its assurance of forgiveness, provided the foundation for Wesley's exceptional self-awareness and persistent self-examination. He could confront his failures and inadequacies with the confidence that God would forgive them and weave them into the fabric of wholeness.

Sanctifying grace is God's presence and power, through the Holy Spirit, to continuously form and shape us in the image of Christ, to perfect us in love, and to create in us "holiness of heart and life." As God's presence and power, through the Holy Spirit, to continuously form us in the image of Christ, sanctifying grace enables us to "go on to perfection" and be all that God created us to be. It is a process of growth as we respond to the means of grace—works of piety and works of mercy. Among the terms Wesley used for the gradual recovery of the likeness of God, or sanctification, was "going on from grace to grace."[25] This understanding of grace as dynamic and continuously transformative was foundational for Wesley's lifelong growth in discipleship and leadership.

This conviction that holiness of heart and life and the restoration of the divine image are God's gift and goal for humanity shaped the Wesleyan class meetings, bands, and conferences. Through practicing the means of grace and "watch[ing] over one another in love,"[26] Wesley and the early Methodists were formed in love for God and neighbor. In being so formed, "the people called Methodists" set out to spread scriptural holiness throughout the lands.

Marks of Leadership Formed by Grace

A fundamental mark of leaders formed by grace is a strong sense of identity as a beloved child of God bearing the imago Dei *and redeemed in Jesus Christ through the Holy Spirit.* Much has been made of John Wesley's experience of assurance and justification on May 24, 1738, as a turning point in his life and ministry, though he did not refer to it as conversion or as pivotal. The experience, however, seemed to have altered his approach from one of earning God's favor to one of living in response to God's grace. Or, whereas justification had been viewed as following sanctification or works worthy of righteousness, now justification preceded sanctification. Rather than working to earn assurance and identity, he devoted his gifts and energies to the restoration of the divine image and growing in the mind of Christ in grateful response to God's grace.

Grace to Lead

Leaders formed by grace see their baptism, not their title or position, accomplishments, or abilities, as the mark of their identity. Their identity is not tied up in the functions they fulfill, including being designated as a leader. They know that their true identity and worth lie in the One to whom they belong and not in what they own or do or know.

Flowing from such an identity is humility, coupled with self-confidence—a trait Jim Collins in his popular book *Good to Great* identifies as a characteristic of "level five leaders." Collins contends that the most effective leaders are a paradoxical blend of strong will and personal humility.[27] Strong commitment to sharing in God's mission and humility emerging from an assurance of identity and worth as a beloved child of God characterize leaders formed by divine grace—God's presence and power active in creating, forgiving, reconciling, and transforming.

Self-awareness characterizes leaders formed by grace. John Wesley's almost obsessive self-examination was part of his ongoing spiritual discipline and formation, and the class meetings and bands provided community contexts for self-examination and confession. As early as the 1730s, Wesley engaged in daily, systematic self-interrogation, in which he identified thoughts and actions that fell short of glorifying God. While such an ascetic approach to self-examination may seem extreme to us, it reflects Wesley's preoccupation with the presence and power of God to create in him "holiness of heart and life."[28] He was keenly aware of the reality of temptations to anger, selfishness, impatience, unfair judgments, sensuousness, and pride. Confronting his own sin and distortion of the *imago Dei* in the context of God's forgiveness and reconciliation was a lifelong component of John Wesley's own formation and leadership.

Academic studies of leadership document the importance of emotional intelligence of leaders; and self-awareness is considered to be the essential component of such intelligence. Stephen R. Covey's widely read book *The 7 Habits of Highly Effective People* is one of many that include self-awareness as definitive for personal growth of leaders.[29] These experts on leadership agree that personal maturity and professional competency require knowledge of one's own identity, personality traits, strengths and weaknesses, gifts and limitations. Effective leaders are sensitive to inner motivations and feelings and the impact they have on relationships and performance of responsibilities.

However, self-awareness and self-examination apart from grace can turn into either an expression of narcissism or self-flagellation. Faithful and effective Christian leaders in the Wesleyan tradition practice self-awareness within the framework of justifying and sanctifying grace. This framework establishes grace as the foundation of one's identity in an awareness of God's love and forgiveness as a beloved child of God. Then, God's power to transform us becomes the source of our giftedness. In the context of God's grace, gifts and strengths are seen as unmerited rather than as achievements; failures and weaknesses are viewed in the light of forgiveness and areas of continued growth.

Leaders formed by grace confess failures and treat mistakes as opportunities for growth. The winter and spring of 1738 were a turning point in the life and leadership of John Wesley. Prior to his missionary journey in Georgia, the young high-achieving and well-educated Anglican priest had succeeded as a student, priest, and university tutor. In Georgia, however, he experienced disappointment as a parish priest, and his ministry among the Native Americans fell short of expectations. He returned to England discouraged and with a sense of lost faith and diminished confidence. His reflective self-examination, personal confessions, and conversations with others such as Peter Böhler paved the way for the assurance, forgiveness, and renewal experienced at Aldersgate Street on May 24. Such persistent confession was part of his formation and leadership throughout his long life.

A persistent temptation of leaders is presumed invincibility and invulnerability. Confession and admitting mistakes are difficult for everyone but particularly for the one who is expected to be more knowledgeable, more mature, more in control—"the leader." Admission of failure is considered weakness and incompetence. The result is defensiveness, self-deception, and resistance to change, and often failures and weaknesses are projected onto others. The leader stymies personal growth and creates a climate in which truth-telling is discouraged.

In his book *The Five Temptations of a CEO: A Leadership Fable*, Patrick M. Lencioni identifies the choice of invulnerability over trust as the fifth temptation of leaders.[30] He affirms that the acknowledgment of our weaknesses and the creation of an atmosphere of truth-telling are essential to effective leadership. An empirical investigation of leadership practices showed that, contrary to the popular notion that apologies signify weakness and undermine confidence in leaders, the leaders who apologize are deemed more transformational than those who do not. The study documents that admission of mistakes, limitations, and failures by the leaders of institutions promotes learning, mitigates against fear of making mistakes, and enables reconciliation within the organization.[31]

Confession in the context of forgiveness and reconciliation is integral to the life and worship of Christians. Acknowledgment of vulnerability and sin is both an expression and a means of grace. Christian leaders in the Wesleyan tradition consider guilt for failure and the desire for forgiveness, reconciliation, and change as a sign of prevenient grace nudging us toward greater wholeness and holiness. Assurance of God's justifying grace provides courage for confronting failure and weakness as a means of continuing growth. Leaders grounded in grace have courage to risk failure in pursuit of the missio Dei, God's salvation of human hearts, communities, nations, and the whole creation.

Leaders formed by grace demonstrate courage in venturing beyond the familiar and into new avenues of mission and ministry. Confidence in the pervasiveness of divine grace—God's presence and power to save and transform—enables us to move beyond our comfort zones and customary patterns. Prevenient grace means that God is already present in our unexplored areas of mission, preparing for new expressions of creativity and renewal. Rather than waiting for the assurance of God's presence, we move forward with confidence that God's presence and power will meet us in the future.

John Wesley's willingness to move out of the familiar and comfortable structures of the university and the local parish and into the mines, the prisons, the open fields, and the hovels of the poor cannot be explained apart from his conviction that God's grace was universally present and available to all. He confronted his own death with the assurance of grace with his last audible words, "The best of all, God is with us."[32]

Sharing in God's mission of salvation requires persistent willingness to move to the margins and toward new frontiers of ministry. At the heart of the missio Dei is the God revealed to Moses: "I have observed the misery of my people who are in Egypt; I have heard their cry on account of their taskmasters. Indeed, I know their sufferings, and I have come down to deliver them" (Ex. 3:7–8). This God was incarnate in Jesus, who so closely identifies with the poor, the imprisoned, and the sick that what is done to them is done unto him and that the final criteria of judgment is our response to "the least of these" (Matt. 25:31–46).

Christian leadership formed by grace, therefore, goes into the hurting, dangerous, and broken places of the world to join God's mission of forgiveness, reconciliation, and transformation. Leaders, pastors and laity, who are faithful to the Wesleyan tradition move to the margins as they participate in God's mission, knowing that God's presence will meet them and that the results do not all depend on their own efforts. We can venture into the unfamiliar with the assurance that we are not alone: "The best of all, God is with us."

Conclusion

Integral to Methodist doctrine and practice is a robust understanding and experience of grace—God's presence and power to create, heal, forgive, reconcile, and transform the entire creation. Grace is unmerited acceptance and unconditional love for individuals, the pardoning of sinners, and the reconciling of persons to God and one another. But grace is more: it is the active presence and power of God at work in the world and in our lives to form us into the mind of Christ and to heal and transform the entire creation into the reign of God brought near in Jesus Christ.

The calling forth, forming, sustaining, and sending of leaders is a work of grace. Leaders grounded in and shaped and sustained by grace root their identity and worth in the *imago Dei*. They exhibit a self-awareness that deals honestly with strengths and weaknesses, successes and failures; and they admit their vulnerability and need for forgiveness, reconciliation, and continued growth. Because of their awareness of the pervasiveness of divine grace, Christian leaders courageously and confidently join God's mission in the margins, ever mindful that they are not alone.

How are persons formed in grace? Like Wesley, persons are formed in grace through experiences and education, as well as courageous decisions informed by one's baptism and Christian vocation to participate in the hopeful vision of God's mission and unfolding reign. What practices nurture and form leaders in grace and enable them to faithfully share in God's mission of salvation? It is to those questions that we now turn.

Questions for Reflection and Discussion

1. What were some of the earliest formational influences on your character and practice of Christian leadership?

2. What are some practices that cultivate in Christian leaders self-awareness and "holiness of heart and life"? What is the relationship between inner holiness and the exercise of leadership in the church and the world?

3. If leadership is a gift of God's grace, what is the role of personal initiative and skill development through education, career advancement, leadership training, the cultivation of institutional and relational connections, and strategic planning?

4. Reflecting on your time as a Christian leader, how have self-awareness, confession, and courage helped you participate and lead the Christian community in God's mission? Were there times when these qualities were not at work? If so, how did this affect your ministry?

Chapter 3

Christian Leadership Sustained by Practices

Christian Leadership as Gift, Not Achievement—The Power of Grace

Starting with God's grace and call upon the lives of Christians is different from starting with an individual's ambition—seeking worldly gain and accumulation of power for selfish and unjust ends. Admittedly, most leadership practice is not the latter, but neither is it necessarily the former. How often does one's identity shift from its proper orientation as a beloved, forgiven child of God to a self-sufficient focus on achievement? How easily does ministry become a means of earning, validating, or proving one's identity and subsequently one's worth, rather than an outpouring of God's work of holiness in and through us? When identity is not grounded in God's unconditional love and invitation, it is all too easy for our ministries, whether lay or ordained, to become competitive, defined by upward mobility and worldly success. When this happens, our rank or title—and even our ordination—can supersede our baptism.

John Wesley's leadership reflects the grace that he persistently preached. Prevenient grace prodded, challenged, guided, and prepared him through his experiences in the Epworth family, his life at Oxford, his journey to and ministry in America, his disciplined pursuit of holiness, and his longing for assurance. His "heart-warming" experience at Aldersgate Street and subsequent confirmation of the message of justification in his visiting the prisons, his field preaching, and his lifelong devotion were lived examples of justifying grace. His growth in understanding, vision, personal holiness, and social transformation testify to the work of sanctifying grace.

Wesley's comprehensive and dynamic understanding and personal experience of grace called forth, shaped, and sustained Wesley as a leader until his death in 1791. It was grace that ignited within him a lifelong desire for "holiness of heart and life" through Christian disciplines and an enduring passion for spreading scriptural holiness over the land. It was grace that enabled him to ignite an evangelistic and missional movement, form institutions, and facilitate leadership in others.

After John Wesley's example, the aim of Christian leadership grounded in grace is to form individuals and communities in holiness of heart and life, so that we may fulfill our callings to enable others to accept the love of God in Christ and participate in the reign of God. Wesley's leadership is inseparable from his Christian vocation, which remained focused upon the "one thing necessary"—restoring the image of God in persons—most often through practicing spiritual disciplines as means of grace.

A Lesson in Leadership: Wesley's "Causes of the Inefficacies of Christianity"

During the last decade of his life, Wesley surveyed and reflected upon the effectiveness of the Methodist movement in England. His reflection went beyond the eighteenth century and raised the question as to why, after eighteen centuries, Christianity had not been more effective in transforming the world. His conclusions have relevance for church leadership in the twenty-first century.

In his sermon "Causes of the Inefficacies of Christianity," Wesley opened with the assertion that Christian communities across the world had done so little good because they produced so few real Christians.[1] Wesley outlined three obstacles that contributed to this plight faced by the church. Christians in such communities often lacked: (1) a sufficient understanding of doctrine; (2) adequate discipline; and/or (3) self-denial.[2]

According to Wesley, an inadequate view of salvation too confined to forgiveness of sins or too narrowly focused upon justification without sanctification nurtured through Christian practices led Christian communities to nurture few real Christians. Apart from practices that form persons and communities in grace and Christlikeness, doctrinal affirmations lose their power to empower and transform. Therefore, Wesley coupled doctrine with practices that shape individuals and communities in accordance with the doctrines.

Wesley's emphasis on disciplines, or Christian practices for cultivating faith, follows Aristotle's guidance for cultivating virtue. Aristotle famously declared in his *Nichomachean Ethics* that a person becomes just by doing just acts, temperate by doing temperate acts, brave by doing brave acts, and so on.[3] To sustain one's identity as a baptized member of the body of Christ and participant in God's reign, one grows in faith by doing faithful acts. Through such disciplined living, Christians are formed in doctrine and actually freed to live more faithfully in the world.

Doctrine

As discussed in Chapter 1, doctrine provides the lens through which we view God, the world, our own identity, the meaning of life, the nature and mission of the Christian community, and the condition and destiny of all existence. Such primary doctrines as the nature and mission of the triune God; human beings as made in the image of God; the distortion and restoration of the divine image; the new creation inaugurated in the life, death, and resurrection of Jesus Christ; and the final consummation of God's reign in Jesus Christ provide the vision and foundation for Christian living and leadership formation. Unfamiliarity with the basic doctrines of the Christian faith results in other lenses through which life is interpreted and formed. Without a firm anchor in Christian doctrine, individual Christians and the church are formed by the prevailing worldview and values of the surrounding culture.

In the modern world, economics and the market represent a dominant lens through which all reality is viewed and evaluated. The market and the values of consumerism, rather than the gospel of Jesus Christ, shape the pervasive logic or vision for ministry today. The global market economy and not the vulnerable, liberating, and suffering God of the Exodus, the cross, and the resurrection has become the dominant god of the modern world. The church itself has become another commodity to be exchanged for self-fulfillment, personal success, institutional advancement, and now even national security.

The basic beliefs that determine our practices become our gods. Underlying the market logic and consumerism are implied beliefs that compete with basic

Christian doctrine. The following are underlying tenets of faith of the market as contrasted with the gospel:

1. The market logic presumes scarcity, while the gospel presumes abundance when the righteousness of God is present.
2. The market measures worth on the basis of its exchange power, while the gospel measures worth in relationship with God's gift and call.
3. The market deals in commodities; the gospel focuses on creation and gift.
4. The market depends on consumption and growth; the gospel depends on relationships and intrinsic value.
5. The market places prime value on efficiency and measurable results; the gospel places prime value on faithfulness to Jesus Christ.
6. The market runs by exchange; the gospel operates by mutuality and shared gift.
7. The market is driven by self-identified needs; the gospel invites participation in God's mission.

The influence of the market's consumerist logic on the church is easy to find. Often theology is quickly replaced by sociology, psychology, and marketing techniques. Pastors look to such disciplines, rather than to theology, Christian tradition, or biblical studies to inform their ministries. The God of Abraham, Isaac, and Jacob; the God of the Exodus; the God of Miriam, Rahab, Elizabeth, and Mary; the God who was in Christ; the crucified God—has become unnecessary, maybe even a hindrance, to leading the institutional church.

Leadership in the church can too often be defined in terms of institutional management and advancement, rather than as a serendipity of discipleship of Jesus Christ. We must not allow the triune God to become another commodity to be marketed by the church in the marketplace of ideas and experiences, rather than the Holy Other (*mysterium tremendum*) before whom the entire cosmos stands in awe, wonder, judgment, and grace.

Not unlike Wesley's observations in his sermon "Causes of the Inefficacies of Christianity," contemporary congregations often demonstrate apathy for sound Christian education and sustained Christian practices—or "discipline," to use Wesley's term—preferring instead techniques promising immediate results.[4] However, John, with Charles, faithfully held the early Methodists to doctrinal and theological accountability. They oversaw the organization of the early Methodist movement with intentional connectedness, not merely to one another for mutual support and accountability but also to the movement's aim to form believers in holiness of heart and life. Wesley consistently urged that authentic spiritual formation could not take place apart from concern for doctrine and, "without society, without living and conversing with [others]."[5]

Discipline

The distinctiveness of the early Methodist movement was not in its novelty or innovation, but in a simple yet profound *integration of doctrine* and discipline toward an authentic Christianity through an intentionally comprehensive program of preaching and small groups. In Wesley's letter to Vincent Perronet, from December 1748, later published as a pamphlet entitled "A Plain Account of the People Called Methodists," he addressed organization and practices of the movement, particularly small-group gatherings for spiritual nurture. In response to pleas for guidance and prayer, Wesley facilitated regular gatherings of interested persons. Only one condition was required of those requesting admission: "a desire to flee from the wrath to come, to be saved from their sins."[6] These gatherings resembled religious societies common within the Church of England, as well as among German pietists, and grew into networks of Methodist circuits across Britain.[7] These "united societies," specifically class meetings alongside penitent, select, and other bands, provided opportunities for early Methodist laypersons, including women, to assume leadership roles such as class and band leaders, lay assistants, stewards, and visitors of the sick.[8]

The General Rules for the United Societies describe the gatherings as "a company of men [and women] having the form and seeking the power of godliness, united in order to pray together, receive words of exhortation, and to watch over one another in love, that they may help each other to work out their salvation."[9] The one condition for admission remained: "a desire to flee from the wrath to come, to be saved from their sins." Continuance in the societies then required a bearing of fruits to that effect facilitated by the following three general rules: (1) by doing no harm, and avoiding evil of every kind; (2) by doing good; and (3) by attending upon the ordinances of God.[10]

The latter consisted of what Wesley often referred to as the means of grace or works of piety and mercy. In the context of bands and classes, individuals encouraged one another in their Christian journeys through public and private prayer, study of Scripture, confession, and fasting, as well as praise and worship. These activities, also known categorically as "works of piety," were means of grace through which individuals might come to know faith in Jesus Christ. Participation in works of piety also provided avenues through which faith might be nurtured and encouraged to grow. Wesley, and other Oxford Methodists, regularly used questions such as the following to assess their spiritual formation:

- Have I prayed with fervor, by myself and at Chapel?
- Have I used the Collects at 9, 12, and 3? Grace?
- Have I after every pleasure immediately given thanks?
- Did I in the morning plan the business of the day?
- Have I been zealous in undertaking and active in doing what good I could?
- Has goodwill been and appeared the spring of all my actions toward others?[11]

In addition to works of piety, members of religious societies, classes, and bands also engaged in "works of mercy," addressing the bodies as well as souls of persons. Whereas works of piety emphasized individual spiritual growth, works of mercy included feeding the hungry, clothing the naked, and visiting the imprisoned, the sick, and the afflicted. Interestingly, Wesley prioritized works of mercy over works of piety to compensate for a perceived reluctance among many Methodists to practice works of mercy.[12]

It may be observed that church membership is not declining in many areas, for example, parts of the Southeast. At the same time, and as many church leaders claim, the church's influence upon people's lives seems to be lessening dramatically. Indeed, according to several respected studies, the majority of Americans claim belief in Christianity; many more claim religious belief in general. This trend may be likened to a vast, shallow swamp. The reason for such an analogy to describe our landscape is that the majority of these Christian believers do not practice their faith in significant depth or with disciplined purpose. Instead, many indulge in an eclectic variety of consumable benefits and services, offered by churches and other religious outlets perpetuating a flooded stagnancy. While there may be much life in a swamp, it is difficult to establish strong roots and branches that produce fruit (John 15:1–8).

In his contemporary classic, *Celebration of Discipline*, Richard Foster builds on this agrarian metaphor, describing spiritual disciplines as similar to cultivating a garden. The garden represents a space cleared and prepared for the planting of God's seeds, followed by the tending of the creative and miraculous growth nurtured by God in Christ through the Holy Spirit.

Spiritual disciplines, or Christian practices, should not be perceived as some dull drudgery aimed at the ceasing of laughter, but rather should be permeated by joy. The purpose of such practices is liberation from slavery to self-interest and fear. Cultivating holiness of heart and life through Christian practices is essential to nurturing faith as a Christian disciple and leader.

Pursuing Christian practices reminds us of our identities, those baptized into the body of Christ and participants in God's reign. Christian practices are not pursued to accomplish a set of tasks or achieve a goal. Neither are they pursued merely by the power of our own will. Holiness of heart and life, cultivated by Christian practices, is a gift from God *in us*—sanctification, imputed righteousness. Christian practices allow us to respond to God's gift of grace in Jesus Christ *for us*—justification, imparted righteousness, opening ourselves to God's ongoing transformation in us. Righteousness is a gift from God. Through Christian practices we are invited to participate in God's reign. In Jesus Christ, through the Holy Spirit, we can receive God's grace and transformation.

Foster used the metaphor of a long, narrow bridge through a deep cavern with sheer drops on either side. The chasm to the right is moral bankruptcy through human strivings for righteousness. This is a heresy of Pelagianism or works of righteousness. The chasm to the left is moral bankruptcy through the absence of human strivings. This is the heresy of antinomianism. The bridge is the path of the spiritual disciplines leading to inner transformation and healing. The path does not produce transformation but places us where transformation can occur.

The Christian transformation occurs over a lifetime of faithful practices; grace-filled leadership is characterized by continual growth and perseverance sustained through disciplined practices and habits. John Wesley's daily disciplines are well documented in his diary and journal. He practiced strict time management long before the phrase was coined. He sought to develop habits that opened him to grace and enabled him to grow into the *imago Dei* and to fully engage his whole being in the *missio Dei*. Through "acts of piety" and "acts of mercy," Wesley and the Methodists established habits designed to form and sustain them in grace, the presence and power of God.

Christian character and leadership are both a gift and a craft. Our identity as beloved and forgiven children of God is a gift from God; living that identity and exhibiting the qualities of the *imago Dei* involves habits formed through persistent practice over time. Freedom to forgive, to love, to welcome the stranger, to experience the presence of God, to appreciate beauty, to be generous and compassionate — requires *practicing* forgiveness, love, hospitality, attentiveness, and giving. Christian leaders, therefore, are both born and grown.

Every form of leadership requires disciplined learning and practice. Only the pianist who learns the musical scales and practices faithfully is free to play a Chopin sonata. Only the gymnast who learns the rules of gymnastics and endures the daily exercises and practices is free to perform on the parallel bars. Only the airline pilot who knows thoroughly the laws of aerodynamics, is completely familiar with the complex instruments of the airplane, and has spent hundreds or thousands of hours practicing aircraft maneuvers, is trusted to fly passengers.

Leaders formed and sustained by grace develop habits that free them to be who they are as sons and daughters of God and to engage all their powers in God's mission of salvation. Growth in discipleship is growth in leadership. Practicing the Wesleyan means of grace is, therefore, an essential leadership development process for those who practice leadership in the Wesleyan tradition.[13]

Self-Denial

A major concern that emerged from John Wesley's review of the effectiveness of the Methodist movement in the eighteenth century was the growing affluence of "the people called Methodists." Rather than increasing generosity, the growing wealth tended to increase pride, self-sufficiency, and neglect of the poor. In "The Causes of the Inefficacy of Christianity," Wesley affirmed that diligence and frugality accompany faithful Christian living and, thereby, tend to make one more prosperous. But as prosperity increases, with its accompanying self-reliance, self-indulgence, and false security, grace decreases. He therefore considered self-denial and generosity as essential practices for Christians to be effective participants in God's mission in the world.

American Christians tend to validate Wesley's concern about the impact of wealth on the health and vibrancy of the spiritual life of disciples of Jesus Christ. A study of Protestant denominations in the United States revealed as much as a 35 percent decline in benevolence giving from 1968 to 1995. As American wealth increased, giving as a percentage of total income declined.[14] Some argue that a postponement of ethical awareness has also occurred, particularly among seeker-oriented congregations, in the midst of an increasingly individualistic and consumer-driven context in which self-sacrifice and community responsibility have become unpopular or at least unneeded.[15]

The Wesleys' context, with the dawning of capitalism and the flourishing of England's colonial trade markets, was not entirely different from contemporary American Protestantism, although most of English society and the majority of Methodists were relatively poor. John Wesley consistently addressed issues of poverty, wealth, and benevolence in his writing. Following scriptural themes, he encouraged generosity among Methodists of every socioeconomic class. Scripture includes 500 verses on prayer, fewer than 500 verses on faith, yet more than 2,000 on money and possessions. Approximately 10 percent (228 verses) of the gospel text focuses on the use of money.[16]

John Wesley was not interested in providing a systematized outline of his own economic ethic. However, by examining oft-repeated themes, Randy Maddox has suggested four cornerstones of John Wesley's message concerning wealth and possessions: (1) The source of all things is God, so all things belong to God. (2) Earthly wealth has been placed in human hands to be stewarded on God's behalf. (3) God expects that we use what we are given to provide for our own necessities and then the necessities of others. (4) To spend our God-given resources on luxuries while others are in need of necessities is to misuse what God has given us.[17]

In his sermon "The Use of Money," John Wesley outlined the proper actions of a Christian approach toward wealth in his famous, and often-misused, injunction: "Gain all you can, without hurting either yourself or your neighbour. . . . Save all you can, by cutting off every expense which serves only to indulge foolish desire. . . . Give all you can, or in other words give all you have to God."[18] This is not, as is sometimes claimed, an endorsement of the laissez-faire capitalism introduced by Adam Smith.[19] John Wesley's writings on similar economic themes, such as *Thoughts on the Scarcity of Provisions* (1773), were roughly contemporary with Smith's publication of *Wealth of Nations* (1776). However, John Wesley and Adam Smith articulated different ultimate goals concerning economics.

Smith advocated the retention of wealth as the basic means of accumulating more wealth. John Wesley encouraged the gaining of wealth so that it could be shared within the kingdom of God.[20] In the sermon "The Use of Money," with the first two points—make all you can and save all you can—Wesley resonates with Smith's advice for individuals to acquire capital. Even on the third point—once wealth has been acquired, it must be used to best advantage—Wesley and Smith agree. However, John Wesley turned this budding economic theory on its head with his last instruction to give all one can. For John Wesley, money is used to best advantage to meet the basic needs of one's neighbor and not simply used as a tool to accumulate more wealth. In a world where the rich get richer, Wesley admonished excess accumulation as theft from God: "Do you not know that God entrusted you with that money (all above what buys necessaries for your families) to feed the hungry, to clothe the naked, to help the stranger, the widow, the fatherless; and indeed, as far as it will go, to relieve the wants of all mankind. How can you, how dare you, defraud your Lord by applying it to any other purpose!"[21]

Wesley had quite a strict definition of wealth, which can be found in his sermon "The Danger of Increasing Riches." In sum, if anyone held goods above the necessities, one was rich. Wesley applied this definition with unyielding strictness, accusing those who accumulated wealth as stealing from the poor.

John Wesley implemented a strict definition of wealth accumulation. Wealth is a gift from God, supplied to humanity to meet basic needs (food, shelter, clothing) and then to be given to others to assist in meeting their basic needs. Wesley saw this ordering not as a viable system of secular communalism but as the requirement of God, lived out in the example of Christ. In his sermon "The Good Steward," Wesley made this connection explicit:

> But first supplying thy own reasonable wants [necessities], together with those of thy family; then restoring the remainder to me [God], through the poor, whom I had appointed to receive it; looking upon thyself as only one of that number of poor whose wants were to be supplied out of that part of my substance which I had placed in thy hands for this purpose; leaving the right of being supplied first, and the blessedness of giving rather than receiving . . . [22]

It is a significant point that one restores the gift of money to God through the poor. Once again Wesley had made clear the spiritual dimension of providing for physical necessities and the physical dimension of the spiritual life and growth. Money is a gift from God that is used for God's purposes. These purposes are outlined in Scripture and modeled in the life of Christ.

Opportunities within the early Methodist movement for demonstrating love of neighbor through works of mercy included charity schools, orphanages, medical clinics, shelters, meals, loans without interest, and other programs to help people meet their most basic needs and to better their condition.[23] Such programs were formed to assist people according to five general categories: (1) the impotent or helpless poor who needed the most basic necessities of food, shelter, and clothing; (2) the unfortunate or able poor who needed assistance in bettering their economic situation; (3) the children who needed education for mind, body, and spirit; (4) the literate but uneducated adults who could benefit from Wesley's publishing program; and (5) the poor and infirm in need of hospitals, pharmacies, and free medical advice. It is important to note that Methodist efforts for assisting the poor initially targeted those within the Methodist societies.[24] This later expanded to some outside the movement through Stranger's Friend Societies.

In keeping with his idea of community after the example of Christ, Wesley encouraged his wealthy patrons not merely to give money to the poor but also to become personally involved with their plight. Miss March, an active and committed Methodist, had well-grounded apprehensions about having physical contact and conversation with the poor. Wesley empathized with her objections but urged her to make such connections after the example of Christ. Wesley was not asking her to befriend the poor but to

> visit the poor, the widow, the sick, the fatherless in their affliction; and this, although they should have nothing to recommend them but that they are bought with the blood of Christ. It is true that this is not pleasing to flesh and blood. There are a thousand circumstances usually attending it which shock the delicacy of our nature, or rather of our education. But yet the blessing which follows this labour of love will more than balance the cross.[25]

Giving to those in need was not just a magnanimous gesture on behalf of the rich to succor the poor; it was a deep spiritual discipline that carried spiritual benefit to both giver and receiver.

Wealthy and poor alike were expected to participate in this discipline. In this way John Wesley universalized the response to poverty. All were expected to offer assistance, including the poor themselves, including the widow with her mites.[26] Added to Wesley's impressive personal record of giving, outlined in detail throughout his diaries, Wesley demanded that his followers give generously and often, even when they themselves stood on the brink of poverty. John Wesley was so bold and so constant in his requests for money to be used on behalf of the poor that Charles Wesley complained: "How many collections think you has my brother made between Thursday evening and Sunday? No fewer than seven. Five this one day from the same poor exhausted people. He has no mercy on them, on the GIVING poor I mean; as if he was in haste to reduce them to the number of the RECEIVING poor."[27]

John Wesley's insistence upon strict financial discipline is arguably one of the primary reasons Methodism did not attract a larger membership during his lifetime.[28] Such strictness eroded slightly over time and was greatly relaxed after John Wesley's death, a situation predicted by Wesley as he neared the end of his life.[29] It does seem that by the 1760s, John Wesley had softened his stance, indicating that it was permissible to accumulate a bit beyond the bare necessities of life, as long as this was not the primary goal being pursued.[30]

Generosity is constitutive of the very meaning of grace, which derives from God's lavish generosity. John Wesley's stewardship of economic resources is rooted in his understanding that all life is a generous gift from God; everything, from our thoughts and personal traits to possessions and influence, is to be used in service to God's mission. Wesley feared that the wealth would lead to a false sense of self-sufficiency and a separation from the poor, which in turn would diminish our reliance on grace. He saw the failure to exercise appropriate stewardship of money as the single most serious threat to the Methodist movement. Hence, he offered as the means of avoiding such a threat his admonition to "gain all you can," "save all you can," and "give all you can." He called the Methodists to earn by contributing to the well-being of others, to save by living simply and avoiding extravagance, and to give by strategically and generously sharing all they had with those in need.

Wesley practiced such generous stewardship throughout his life and even in his death.[31]

Generosity of spirit is a common trait of effective leaders as identified in the growing leadership literature. Openness to the contributions of colleagues, expressions of gratitude and praise, willingness to share credit for accomplishments, and sharing of authority are seen as evidences of generosity among leaders. Such generosity fosters morale among colleagues, enhances motivation, encourages creative risk-taking, increases cooperation, and strengthens community.

Leaders who are formed and sustained by grace cultivate attentiveness to God's generosity through practicing the means of grace and all of life as a gift to be used in service to God's mission. They guard against the seduction of privilege and wealth as signs of their superior gifts or rewards for their achievements. They view their work as a means of adding to the well-being of others. They live simply and shun extravagance and opulence, and they give generously and strategically of financial resources. One such leader who lives on 10 percent of her income and contributes 90 percent to such causes as endowed scholarships for needy students and multiple benevolent causes through her local church explained her generosity this way: "Everything I have is a trust from God and I am privileged to be able to share in what God is doing in the world." That is leadership formed and sustained by grace!

A Case Study from Methodism's History

Interweaving doctrine, discipline, and self-denial in leadership formation and practice presents particular challenges. While we have focused primarily on growth in grace, it may be worth stating that there is nothing wrong with numerical growth. Ultimately, the message of salvation is good news that results in the expansion of the reign of God. However, leadership that focuses so narrowly upon quantitative growth, specifically congregational membership, reveals a myopia that overlooks the true *telos* of the gospel of Jesus Christ, namely, the reign of God. A further bereavement occurs when, in their desire to add members, many local churches look only to similar demographics and/or similar or higher social status, neglecting Jesus' ministry to the marginalized, including children, the infirm, and the impoverished.[32]

All this to say that "growth" in early Methodism did take account of numbers but remained primarily focused upon growth in grace, most often addressed to those on the margins of society through relationship with God and neighbor in the unfolding reign of God. The interconnectedness of field preaching among the marginalized of society with small-group nurture facilitated a steady, and sometimes slow, growth in the early Methodist movement that emerged from doctrinal foundations of grace.

The Methodist renewal movement began modestly early in 1739 in Bristol with the inauguration of field preaching by George Whitefield among the coal miners of Kingswood, soon followed by class meetings.[33] Upon Whitefield's invitation, John Wesley arrived in Bristol in late March 1739 to take Whitefield's place among the societies. When Wesley learned of Whitefield's preaching in the open air, he wrote that he could "scarce reconcile [himself] at first to this strange way of preaching in the fields." While open-air preaching, often called "field preaching" (though not necessarily limited to fields, as it could include venues from market squares to gallows), was not illegal, it was highly irregular, especially among respectable Anglican clergy. John Wesley claimed he had been "so tenacious of every point relating to decency and order that [he] should have thought the saving souls almost a sin if it had not been done in a church."[34]

However, Jesus' Sermon on the Mount, John Wesley's text for April 1st, provided a persuasive precedent, together with his witnessing Whitefield preach to approximately 30,000 people.[35] The following afternoon, Wesley "submitted 'to be more vile'" and preached in the open air to—by his estimate— 3,000 to 4,000. During his first month in Bristol, John Wesley estimated a total attendance of 47,500 persons at his field preaching, an average of 3,000 per event.[36] Field preaching and additional opportunities to preach out of doors allowed Wesley, among others, to reach large numbers often consisting of those marginalized by society, such as the poor and outcast.

Despite the staggering numbers reported at such gatherings, in 1744 John Wesley cautioned against excessive field preaching as his leadership turned to consolidating the movement and creating a foundation of doctrine and discipline.[37] As Heitzenrater observes, the aim of John Wesley's leadership of the early Methodist renewal movement to "spread scriptural holiness" was not to create a "wildfire" but, rather, to manage an intentional and steady pace of growth.[38]

Although Whitefield and the Wesleys' preaching, particularly in the open air, is well documented for its evangelistic impact upon British as well as North

American Christianity, their preaching did not stand alone as an effective method of evangelism. In 1745, the Methodist Conference under John Wesley's leadership decided to experiment with preaching wherever opportunities arose, first in Wales and Cornwall, and then later in the north, without forming societies (or regardless of the presence of societies), to nurture those responding.[39] The results of the experiment were unequivocal. Christian formation provided by the Methodist small groups that John Wesley organized allowed a significant number of those moved by the revival's preaching to be nurtured and maintained in the faith.[40] When these groups were not accessible, those moved by the preaching were often lost. The experiment ceased in 1748, and the Conference turned its focus to the formation of societies.[41]

In his "A Plain Account of the People Called Methodists," John Wesley described the emergence of the early Methodist renewal movement with little if any reference to quantitative growth. Instead, the document tracked a rich tapestry of themes embodied by and characteristic of the movement, namely, theology, organization, and mission growing from a shared commitment to "spreading scriptural holiness."

It is important to remember that Methodism began as a movement among the poor of eighteenth-century England, and John Wesley considered friendship with and aid to the poor as an essential spiritual discipline. While his ministry among those on the margins was a means of grace to the poor, the imprisoned, the sick, and the children, his relationships with them were means of grace to Wesley. Through such relationships, Wesley *experienced* God's presence and power to redeem and transform persons; and he witnessed the impact of the gospel on the lives of those deemed worthless and without hope, including the condemned malefactors on their way to the gallows. Such experiences confirmed to Wesley the validity of the gospel of salvation by grace through faith. His lifelong relationships with and commitment to the poor shaped his vocational choices, his vision for ministry, and his strategies for participation in God's mission.

Holding together and interweaving doctrine, discipline, and self-denial helped Wesley avoid a persistent challenge of leaders. Positions of leadership and power tend to separate us from those without power and position. Leaders frequently live in "bubbles" with other leaders and spend their time with people like themselves. Leadership is often accompanied by privileges and choices that enable the leaders to escape the challenges and struggles of ordinary folks. Many leaders admit to the difficulty in having people tell them the truth, especially regarding their own failures and inadequacies. Leaders can thereby develop a false sense of invincibility and an inability to identify with the very people with whom they have leadership responsibilities.

We have experienced in recent times the tragic consequences of leaders who lose touch with those who live on the margins of society—the poor, the immigrants, the imprisoned, the diseased, those whom Jesus called "the least of these" and Charles Wesley called "Jesus' bosom friends." Political and governmental leaders enact laws and policies that protect the privileges of those already advantaged, while neglecting those without the necessities needed to flourish as beloved children of God. Corporate financial and business executives engage in practices that result in creating huge disparities of resources and enable "the rich to get richer while the poor get poorer." Church leaders often lose touch with "the people in the pews" and develop denominational systems that no longer embody the gospel of radical hospitality that includes the outcasts, the orphans, the widows, and the sojourners.

Leaders formed and sustained by grace develop friendships across the boundaries of race, class, ethnicity, and privilege. Such leaders cultivate the ability to recognize and receive the gifts of those who are different from themselves. They avoid using the poor, the imprisoned, and the vulnerable as mere objects of charity or as means to their own enrichment. Rather, through the lens of Jesus Christ, they see the marginalized as brothers and sisters, equally made in the image of God, and with gifts for participation in God's mission. A great, untapped resource for understanding and practicing leadership in the Wesleyan tradition is the gift of wisdom and grace found among those who live on the margins of society.

Community as the Context for Sound Doctrine and Christian Practice

Central to the vitality of early Methodism was the focus on community. The leadership of John and Charles Wesley cannot be understood apart from their strong commitment to the church and the importance of small groups of support and accountability. They presumed the sacraments and practices of the Anglican Church as essential for Christian formation. Their efforts were directed toward renewing the church, and the forming of societies, classes, and bands as communities of mutual support and accountability characterized their leadership. It was primarily in small groups that the early Methodists experienced their "hearts strangely warmed"; and it was in such communities of support and accountability that they grew in grace and mission. It was in small groups that leaders were identified, called forth, taught, formed, deployed, and sustained. John Wesley's own leadership was inseparable from his ongoing relationships with other leaders such as his brother Charles, his mother Susanna, Peter Böhler, George Whitefield, John Fletcher, Mary Bosanquet, and numerous others with whom he worked and engaged in ongoing conversation.

Just as Wesley affirmed that no one can be a Christian alone, no one can be a leader in isolation from a community of support and accountability. The image of the charismatic individual leader is increasingly questioned in the leadership literature. It has been a popular image in American society, including the church. Companies, institutions, and churches long assumed that the solution to success was a leader who would provide the vision, strategy, and motivation necessary for flourishing. While the individual leader is critically important, a quality of effective leadership identified in most leadership studies is a sense of shared responsibility, support, and accountability. Mutuality trumps individuality, and community supersedes isolation.

Isolation, loneliness, and unrealistic expectations represent ongoing temptations for leaders. Pastors are particularly susceptible to such enticements. Diminished effectiveness, impaired relationships, depression, and lost passion for ministry are among the potential consequences. Peer relationships characterized by honesty, vulnerability, acceptance, and mutual accountability promote learning, confession, healing, creativity, and hope. The early Methodist class meetings and bands and contemporary covenant discipleship groups offer a model for contemporary leaders who are formed and sustained by grace.

Discipleship and Leadership Formed and Sustained by Christian Practices

As John Wesley was concerned about the causes of "the inefficacy of Christianity" and the perceived lack of effectiveness of the Methodists of eighteenth-century England, so are we concerned about the faithfulness and fruitfulness of heirs of Wesley in the twenty-first century. John and Charles Wesley, however, provide an example of leadership formed in sound doctrine and faithful practices that laid the foundation for the remarkable growth of Methodism throughout the world.

As John and Charles Wesley clearly demonstrated, Christian discipleship precedes and produces leadership. Discipleship—as well as leadership—includes belief (doctrine) and practices (discipline). Doctrine and discipline are inextricably connected in the Wesleyan tradition. Doctrine provides the lens through which we perceive the world and the framework by which we derive meaning and purpose, specifically the church's mission in the world. Discipline consists of the practices that form us more deeply in accordance with this worldview and invite our participation in God's reign.

However, practices are means of formation—avenues of God's grace—not ends in themselves or ways of earning God's favor or achieving success. They are means of receiving and cultivating God's gifts of discipleship and leadership. Through Christian practices, we affirm and participate in the transformative power of divine grace and engage in practices that sensitize us to God's presence and power. By participating in Christian practices that serve as means of God's grace, we are freed to be who God intends us to be and to fully participate with our whole being in God's mission for the church in the world toward the salvation of the cosmos. In so doing, we share in the gift of leadership made possible by grace.

Questions for Reflection and Discussion

1. How can Christian leaders cultivate a generosity of spirit? Is this an attribute you would use to describe yourself? What are some barriers to generosity in our culture and the church, and how can leaders overcome such barriers?

2. What measures other than numerical growth must Christian leaders focus on? What forms of growth have you focused on in the past? What steps could you take in order to broaden the focus in the future?

3. Why did John Wesley work to form relationships with people who had little visible power or leadership potential?

4. How does the emphasis on mutuality and shared responsibility enable the leader to avoid the "leadership bubble" and maximize the contributions of others? How are mutuality and shared responsibility connected with God's mission of salvation?

Chapter 4

Contemporary Challenges and Opportunities

Many qualities needed in a Christian leader transcend time and culture: a sense of identity as a beloved and forgiven child of God; integrity grounded in commitment to holiness of heart and life; self-awareness emerging from repentance and forgiveness; vision centered in the *missio Dei*; and hope anchored in the coming reign of God. Nevertheless, all leadership takes place in particular contexts, and the qualities and skills necessary in different times and cultures vary in their expression and application. While God's grace is the underlying reality that forms disciples and leaders across time and cultures, grace is also incarnate in specific times and places.

The Wesleyan movement originated in the midst of the particular challenges and opportunities of eighteenth-century British culture. Among the challenges confronting the Church of England during this time were the Enlightenment, with its rationalism and emerging scientific worldview; the Industrial Revolution and emerging capitalism, accompanied by growing urbanization and economic disparity; the slave trade and its dehumanization and human exploitation; the decline of British hegemony and resulting revolution; and the elitist captivity of the established church, with its separation from the masses, particularly the poor and working class.

According to John Wesley, God raised up "the people called Methodists" to be a renewal movement on behalf of God for the salvation of human hearts, communities, nations, and the entire creation. John and Charles Wesley, as well as many others, were called forth and formed to lead this evangelical and missional movement amid the formidable challenges. Central to the effectiveness of the early Methodists was their profound experience and robust understanding of grace. It was grace that sent them across the British Isles and beyond with a passion "to reform the nation[s], particularly the Church; and to spread scriptural holiness over the land[s]."[1]

There are many parallels between the challenges and opportunities confronted by the Methodists of the eighteenth century and those faced by their descendants in the twenty-first century. There are also unique realities today that require particular qualities and skills as expressions of leadership faithful to the Wesleyan tradition. Let us explore some of the challenges and opportunities, and the leadership needed to confront them.

Competing Worldviews

The Bible and Christian tradition no longer provide the primary framework for forming the life and structure of contemporary culture in the United States. Theology is no longer seen as the "queen of the sciences" by which all truth is determined. The dominant prescientific worldview and cosmology of the Bible seem quaint and outdated to many, if not most, who live in the United States, including those who identify themselves as Christians. Indeed, images of a three-storied universe, with the earth being the center, the forces of nature being the expressions of God's intervention, and everything from the weather to personal physical healing being interpreted as divine acts, are relegated to the margins of contemporary North American culture.

When knowledge of Scripture and Christian tradition wanes, different narratives easily supplant the worldview formed by the story of the triune God's mighty acts of salvation. The theme of the Christian worldview is God's grace expressed in the creation of the universe, the calling and forming of a people to be light to the nations, and the deliverance of the Hebrew slaves from captivity and their restoration from exile. Central to this story is God coming in human form in Jesus the Christ, who was crucified and resurrected as the firstborn of a new creation and who, through the Holy Spirit, brought the church into being as a visible herald, sign, foretaste, and instrument of God's present and coming reign of justice, compassion, generosity, peace, and joy. Christian leaders today serve in a culture in which such a story is unfamiliar to many, inside and outside the church.

Science has become a prevailing lens for the formation of a worldview and a framework for understanding and structuring life. Biology, chemistry, physics, astronomy, and mathematics are the "royal family" of the sciences. They inform the understanding of reality, from the nature of human existence to the processes of the natural order and the structure of the limitless universe. God as a primary or sole explanation of the origin and nature of life and the source of meaning, purpose, and destiny has been moved to the margins in the contemporary context. Reason and the scientific method are looked to for the explanations of life's puzzles and solutions to vexing problems. Science has made more challenging the psalmist's question: "When I look at your heavens, the work of your fingers, the moon and stars that you have established; what are human beings that you are mindful of them, mortals that you care for them?" (Ps. 8:3–4). A view of the heavens, the moon and stars, as creations of a personal God who "marks even a sparrow's fall"[2] cannot be presumed in the contemporary context; and Christian leaders function within the context of a scientifically and technologically oriented worldview.

Added to the "hard sciences" as primary sources for shaping contemporary worldviews are the social sciences—sociology, psychology, economics, and political science. Human conditions and interactions once accounted for in theological language and categories are now explained with the tools of psychology and sociology. Traditional theological concepts such as sin, salvation, atonement, reconciliation, and grace are no longer in the vocabulary of the general population as descriptions of the human condition and its transformation. The church itself is increasingly understood primarily in sociological categories and described in terms of its organizational structure, membership demographics, institutional systems, and statistical characteristics. Biblical and theological images of the church and its mission are either presumed or ignored in many discussions of the church's nature. Renewal efforts tend to rely more on the tools of the social sciences and marketing than on the frameworks of soteriology and ecclesiology.

Economic ideology and determinism also offer an alternative worldview that challenges the Christian gospel. When reality is viewed through the lens of economics, everything becomes a commodity and is valued in accordance with its exchange rate in the marketplace. The earth itself is reduced to utilitarian function, resulting in the exploiting and depleting of natural resources, polluting the earth, endangering the ecological balance, and jeopardizing the entire planet. Necessities for human thriving, such as food, water, shelter, medicine, and education, become products available only to those with adequate financial resources. Institutions, including churches, depend upon the survival of the economically fittest. In an economically deterministic worldview, the *telos* of institutions is shaped by what is profitable in the marketplace. Scientific research is controlled by funding sources, the curricula of educational institutions shaped in accordance with market forces, and political power controlled by those with economic means. Human worth and dignity rooted in identity as a beloved and forgiven child of God are replaced by personal worth dependent upon productivity and the accumulation of material goods. In such a world, the notion that life and all existence is a generous gift from God and that divine grace is the determinative force at work in history runs counter to the prevailing worldview forged by economic ideology and determinism.

The limits of science, technology, and economics to define reality and solve problems are becoming increasingly evident. Apart from a comprehensive vision of life's purpose, science threatens rather than enhances existence. Paradoxically, all advances in science and technology are accompanied by adverse unplanned consequences. The chemical and biological revolutions have made possible improved health *and* a destructive drug culture. Advances in physics have enabled travel to distant places and produced weapons of mass destruction with potential for cataclysmic devastation. Computer and communication technology have multiplied information *and* expanded access to pornography, slander, and propaganda. Further, we know that the deepest longings of the human spirit and requirements for thriving, such as meaning, purpose, community, love, and hope, cannot be met by advances in science and technology.

The global financial crises of 2008 and 2009 have thrown into stark relief the limitations of market economics to provide security and well-being. No economic system offers salvation, and unchecked consumerism destroys the very institutions it creates. Without the guidance of a *telos* that includes justice, compassion, and accountability—which protect the least and most vulnerable—economic systems exploit the weak, devastate the earth and its resources, and contribute to violence and destruction within the human family. The validity of Jesus' warnings is substantiated in the contemporary world: "Take care! Be on your guard against all kinds of greed; for one's life does not consist in the abundance of possessions" (Luke 12:15); "You cannot serve God and wealth" (Luke 16:13).

Christian leaders in the twenty-first century have the unparalleled opportunity to articulate a framework for a worldview comprehensive and coherent enough to marshal the gifts of science and economics toward God's salvation of the entire cosmos. The sciences and economic systems are gifts of God and integral to the flourishing of creation. However, they are also insufficient as sole frameworks for a faithful and coherent worldview. For the first time in human history, science and technology have made available the ability to eliminate hunger, poverty, and most childhood diseases. The church is uniquely positioned to provide a moral framework and vision sufficiently comprehensive and coherent to marshal the resources of science and economics toward the reign of God. Christian leaders are needed to shape communities of faith and institutions in accordance with God's holistic salvation—leaders formed and transformed by God's grace in Jesus Christ through the Holy Spirit.

Disestablishment of the Church

Challenges

The statistical decline of membership in mainline denominations, including The United Methodist Church, signals a shift in the religious landscape of society in the United States. This shift represents a formidable challenge to Christian leadership in the twenty-first century. For centuries, Western culture and Christendom have existed as integral components of the same reality. Evidence now abounds that such an arrangement is coming to an end.[3] Christianity is now one option among many in the marketplace of worldviews; and the church is no longer viewed as a privileged institution in democratic societies. Even in the early history of the United States, with established churches such as the Anglican, Roman Catholic, Dutch Reformed, Baptist, and Quaker congregations, citizenship and church membership coexisted; later, in the mid-twentieth century, the majority of persons living in the United States were at least sympathetic to the church. However, in the early years of the new century, there is significantly less popular support for the institutional church.

The marginalization of Christianity and churches is most evident in Europe. Yet in the United States, the signs of diminished influence and cultural disestablishment of the Christian churches are becoming increasingly apparent, resulting in a growing sense of crisis among church leaders. Churches bemoan the loss of denominational identity and loyalty and scramble to stop the membership hemorrhage and financial shortfalls. Some leaders and groups have turned to political action as the primary means of maintaining and restoring the United States as "a Christian nation." A survival mentality dominates the mood of many judicatories, local churches, and pastors who are moving church-growth strategies and marketing techniques to the center of the church's life. Techniques and tactics for institutional success have taken on added prominence in discussions among church leaders.

The disestablishment of the church in North American society significantly impacts the expectations and morale of church leaders. Statistical decline and loss of institutional influence in the broader culture contribute to feelings of failure and ineffectiveness by those responsible for leading such institutions. The demands of competing worldviews and difficulty in interpreting the gospel in the complex world dominated by science, technology, economics, and political power burden and stress Christian leaders. Judicatory leaders, such as bishops and district superintendents, add another layer of quantifiable expectations and evaluations to the internal expectations and self-evaluations of pastors and other church leaders.

What characterizes and sustains Christian leadership and ministry in a culture where the church is disestablished? What is the basic *Telos* of Christian leadership? How do quantifiable outcomes relate to discipleship, changed hearts and lives, and prophetic influence on societal issues? What temperaments and skills are needed for leadership in an often-marginalized church? What is the relationship between practices that form and sustain persons in grace and leadership development and morale? These are among the critical questions that confront Christian leaders in the twenty-first century.

Opportunities

The disestablishment of the mainline church may represent a unique opportunity for the church to recover its identity and mission as an alternative community in the world but not of it. While many see the loss of cultural prominence as a threat to the church, it may be an occasion for reclaiming theological and missional identity and purpose. Charles Bayer sees the demise of Christendom as an opportunity for "discover[ing] and liv[ing] into a new ecclesial paradigm." In this paradigm, Bayer says, the church views its cultural and religious marginalization as an act of Providence, since the church is now given the opportunity to recover the original context of its mission and ministry: the margins, with and on behalf of the marginalized.[4] Hendrik Pieterse adds that by turning toward the margins, the church "can grasp for our day the simple but profound truth . . . the church's healing into faithfulness lies in the company of those despised, marginalized, and excluded."[5]

The margins are an appropriate and even essential location for the church. The disestablishment of the church in North American society is an opportunity to reclaim an ecclesial identity and purpose within the *missio Dei* to serve all of creation, including those on the margins of society. It is from the margins that the church bears witness to the God of the Exodus and of Jesus Christ. It is among the vulnerable, the oppressed, the poor, the imprisoned, the sick, and the pushed-aside that the church is a visible sign, foretaste, and instrument of God's new creation. The church is most fully the church when it joins God on the margins and embraces ministry to and with "the least of these."

As an alternative community within the larger society, the church in its life and practice is a marginalized people.[6] Claiming our identity as a community on the margins of the world within God's reign is a more faithful response to disestablishment than being so incorporated in society that the church has no distinctive qualities apart from the broader culture. Only by claiming identity and mission on the margins can the church be an agent of reconciliation and transformation. The challenge and opportunity confronting those called to lead the church are to claim the church's identity as a marginalized community and to engage the people who live on the margins of society—the poor, the imprisoned, the immigrants, the abused, and the vulnerable.

After the example of John Wesley and the early Methodist movement (also a marginalized community, particularly in its earliest embodiments), relationships among rich and poor, powerful and powerless were valued as a component of Christian discipleship and formation. Those with wealth and capital worked alongside those without influence or means, facilitating opportunities for economic development consistent with the gospel, as well as sanctification for all. Marginalization of the church and its disestablishment from its influence in the contemporary context is not necessarily a vow of poverty or reclusion. It is an opportunity to faithfully steward wealth, influence, and power, and to share the gospel in and through communities of mutual accountability in response to God's rich gift of grace in Jesus Christ.

Pluralism, Diversity, and Polarization

Challenges

Another challenge and opportunity confronting Christian leaders in the twenty-first century are the realities of pluralism, diversity, and polarization. The church no longer exists in homogenous communities where everyone shares common beliefs, heritages, and practices. Almost every city, town, and village includes people representing a variety of ethnic, racial, religious, political, and cultural traditions and characteristics. Contemporary communication and mobility transport people and cultures across traditional geographic and national boundaries. What once seemed "foreign" and inaccessible now enters our living rooms through television, and those who seemed a world away from us often live next door.

In an earlier era, "other religions" meant Baptists, Methodists, Presbyterians, Episcopalians, Pentecostals, Catholics, and a few Jews. Today Muslims, Buddhists, Hindus, avowed atheists and agnostics, and a plethora of religious and spiritual adherents work and live in communities alongside Protestant and Catholic Christians and Reformed and Orthodox Jews. All of the diverse populations bring their own worldviews, sacred writings, and liturgical practices to the cultural mix, and many compete for the claim of supremacy and ultimate truth.

Even within traditions, stark differences exist, often erupting into conflict and violence. Sunnis versus Shiites, Protestants versus Catholics, and conservatives versus liberals express the polarization within religious traditions. Conflicts and controversies over volatile moral, ethical, and political issues threaten to split many Protestant denominations, including The United Methodist Church. Homosexuality, abortion, gender roles, capital punishment, war, patriotism, worship styles, authority of Scripture, and qualifications for ordination are but a few of the issues that create clashes within local congregations and denominations, often resulting in splits and animosity within families and communities and impacting the way leaders understand their role and the church's ministry.

Pluralism and diversity create challenges for leaders of congregations and institutions. Conflicts require significant investment of energies and attention by leaders and often divert attention from the larger mission of the church. Additionally, statistical growth and measurable results become more difficult when tensions and disputes exist within congregations and denominations. Leaders are tempted to avoid controversial subjects and concerns in order to preserve harmony and to avoid risking decline in membership support. The prophetic dimension of Christian Scripture and tradition is deemphasized or silenced altogether as a subtle tool for institutional growth.

Opportunities

Conflict, controversy, and differences offer an opportunity for growth in Christian discipleship and a deeper understanding of love of God and neighbor. Conflict, controversy, and difference are significant parts of the church's tradition. Much of the New Testament, particularly the letters of Paul, was written in response to clashes of cultures, traditions, theological perspectives, and cultic practices. The core doctrines of justification by faith and God's reconciliation of humanity through Jesus Christ emerged in the midst of polarization and division. The church was birthed in diversity as the Holy Spirit descended on the gathering of the assorted nations and languages and ethnicities gathered in Jerusalem at Pentecost, and a new gift of unity and understanding was experienced. While not every confrontation in church tradition has ended in harmony and reconciliation (indeed, there are terrible wounds that may not be healed until the eschaton), when we confront the "other," we learn more about ourselves and about God and God's relationship to creation.

Indeed, reconciliation is at the heart of the church's mission, as Paul affirmed to the polarized Corinthian congregation: "[I]n Christ God was reconciling the world to himself, . . . and entrusting the message of reconciliation to us" (2 Cor. 5:19). In Christ, God has already reconciled all things and called the church to be a sign and means of that reconciliation. Consequently, conflict and differences represent opportunities for the church to embody the grace that reconciles and creates community among diverse people.

Practices of confession, forgiveness, and reconciliation can be a powerful evangelistic witness. Unity in the midst of diversity thereby becomes a sign of God's new community in which "there is no longer Jew or Greek, there is no longer slave or free, there is no longer male and female; for all of you are one in Christ Jesus" (Gal. 3:28). Leading the church to be a community of confession, forgiveness, and reconciliation in a diverse and polarized world is a particular challenge and opportunity in the twenty-first century. United Methodists with the Wesleyan emphasis on "catholic spirit" have a rich, if at times complex, heritage on which to draw for such leadership.

Individualism and Loss of Community

Challenges

Rugged individualism has been a valued attribute in the United States since immigrants first arrived in the new land. The adventurous settlers established a new nation and created a constitution and system of government in support of the freedoms and rights of individuals. Personal initiative, ambition, ingenuity, and inventiveness account for many remarkable contributions to human progress in North America. Individual dignity and personal responsibility are noble values that merit preservation and enhancement.

Individualism, however, can elevate individual autonomy and personal interests to the level of idolatry, thereby fragmenting community. The individual's self-interests are advanced at the expense of the common good. Personal happiness and fulfillment become the ultimate goal, and everything is evaluated in terms of the contribution to that goal. Support of and accountability to others are contingent upon whether these practices promote the self-identified goal of personal fulfillment and happiness, resulting in weakened community ties and increased isolation.

The loss or fragmenting of community is well documented by social scientists such as Robert Putnam. In his groundbreaking book *Bowling Alone: The Collapse and Revival of American Community,* Putnam documents how we have become increasingly disconnected from family, friends, neighbors, and democratic structures.[7] Participation in collective activities and organizations, such as bowling leagues and civic groups, has declined and given way to individual sports and activities.

The impact of individualism on the church in the United States is pervasive and systemic. The church is one voluntary organization among many competing for the loyalties and commitments of individuals. Individuals choose churches on the basis of personal preferences and self-identified needs and expectations. Pastoral leaders know that unless they fulfill the expectations of the persons in the congregation, those persons will likely exercise the option of choosing another church. The notion of being part of a covenant community of mutual mission, ministry, support, and accountability is foreign to many who participate in North American churches. Even *corporate* worship may be more accurately described as a collection of individuals having private devotions together.

Individualism contributes to a distortion of the Christian gospel when it limits God's salvation to personal conversion and neglects the power of divine grace to transform institutions, nations, cultures, and systems. The bifurcation of the gospel into "personal" and "social" reflects such a distortion. There is only one gospel, with inseparable personal and social dimensions. Justification, for example, includes both pardon of the individual and incorporation into Christ's body, the church.

Accompanying individualism and the loss of community is a perception of leadership that emphasizes the role of the individual leader above the corporate or leadership of the community. Institutions, including the church, assume that the exceptionally gifted individual will provide the necessary vision, motivation, strategy, and process for moving forward. When problems arise or progress lags behind expectations, a new leader is sought. United Methodism's itinerant system of pastoral leadership is particularly susceptible to the assumption that a change of pastors is the key to quantifiable measures of success.

Another adverse consequence of individualism and its impact on leadership is a lack of awareness of the influence of systems and structures on individuals. The concept of systemic realities, including structural sin, gives way to assigning all problems to individual attributes, decisions, and actions. A growing body of scholarship, however, substantiates the interconnectedness of the personal and the social. Individuals are born and formed in families, neighborhoods, and institutions. Individuals are influenced by cultural, social, economic, and political forces beyond their total control. Leaders are formed within such systems and structures, and they function with them. Leaders both influence the systems and structures and are influenced by them. The entire system is an organism that functions corporately in the broader society. In other words, institutions and structures *lead*.

Opportunities

There are growing signs of a reemerging longing for community, and therein lies an opportunity for the church and its leaders. Though some would argue for the Internet's contribution to isolation and loss of community, others claim that the Internet is experiencing a mushrooming of connecting sites in which strangers reach out in virtual reality for relationships and friendships. Neighborhoods are constructed and marketed as "planned communities," offering gathering places for families and individuals. Support groups are growing for persons with common addictions, struggles, and interests. Churches are opening their doors for such groups and creating small groups for Bible study, discipleship formation, and missional involvement. Evangelistic ministries continue to reach out to individuals while also incorporating persons into communities and networks of discipleship. This is a wonderful opportunity for United Methodists to recover a contemporary version of class meetings, bands, and societies devoted to discipleship formation.

The social sciences and leadership studies that address how systems and organizations function provide the church with important tools for institutional transformation and mission. Systems thinking and organizational analyses, however, need theological grounding and interpretation. Rather than opting for the language and images of the social sciences, Christian leaders have such theologically rich images as "body of Christ," "new creation," "people of God," "royal priesthood," and "holy nation" as the framework for understanding the nature and mission of the church. Serious theological reflection will enable the insights from the social sciences and leadership studies to be used as tools for enhancing the leadership of communities as well as individuals.

Qualities and Skills Needed to Address Challenges and Opportunities

The challenges and opportunities confronting leaders in the twenty-first century call for leaders, both individual and corporate, with particular qualities and skills. The challenges of competing worldviews, the disestablishment of the church, pluralism, diversity, and polarization, as well as individualism and loss of community, have few parallels in history from which we can learn. However, the contemporary context highlights particular qualities and skills inspired by the Wesleyan tradition for Christian leaders to maximize participation in God's mission of salvation.

Foundation repair and reinforcement is a necessary task of leaders in the twenty-first century. Effective leadership amid competing and conflicting worldviews requires a deep grounding in Scripture and the Christian tradition. Church leaders must address immediately and comprehensively the erosion of basic knowledge of Scripture and the doctrines and traditions of the Christian faith by those within the church. Otherwise, the competing worldviews will render our witness ineffectual and the church's participation in God's mission tepid. Without a solid theological foundation, efforts to revitalize and renew declining membership will be short-lived programmatic structures built on sand rather than the solid rock of the gospel.

We have a precedent in the early Methodist movement. John and Charles Wesley and their coworkers laid a foundation for the subsequent growth of the Methodists. Despite staggering numbers of listeners in open-air preaching, the early Methodist movement showed a relatively slow growth through an intense process of Christian formation in small-group gatherings resulting in changed lives. Priority was given to recovering "primitive Christianity" through teaching, preaching, writing, and practices that formed individuals and groups in accordance with holiness of heart and life. John Wesley's extensive written and oral sermons, as well as tracts, letters, and treatises, were directed toward laying a foundation in Scripture and tradition upon which the societies, classes, bands, evangelistic strategies, and mission engagement were built.

Charles Wesley's poems and hymns became a repository of theological interpretation, Christian formation, and evangelical and missional motivation, as well as vehicles of worship. They laid a foundation from which we benefit and upon which we continue to build.

Ron Heifetz distinguishes between two leadership challenges: technical and adaptive.[8] A *technical* challenge is a problem for which there is an immediate and known solution. For example, a blocked artery can be treated with medication, a stent, or bypass surgery. An *adaptive* challenge is one for which no known solution currently exists and that requires a cultural shift. Thus, while a blocked artery calls for a technical response, heart health requires a lifestyle change. In the context of church leadership, membership decline can be treated as a technical challenge: one can deal with it by developing and implementing a marketing plan for recruitment. However, if renewal of the congregation through transformed lives is the challenge, then a cultural shift is necessary that will include education and formation over an extended period of time.

John Wesley approached the early Methodist renewal movement as an adaptive challenge, which required laying a foundation and a lifetime of practices. Contemporary heirs of the early Methodists confront the need for a cultural shift in the church's life. Leaders, therefore, must address the immediate technical challenges with an eye on the long-range cultural shift necessary. Foundation repair requires patience and perseverance and a willingness to get one's hands dirty and work without recognition and immediate visible results.

A comprehensive vision of God's holistic salvation is required of leadership that meets the challenges of the twenty-first century. Christian leadership has always lived with the tension between the *already* and *not yet* dimensions of God's salvation and reign. Eschatology is an essential component of Christian leadership aimed to meet the challenges of the twenty-first century. We celebrate the kingdom of God already present, and we anticipate its completion. It is the vision of a new creation brought to fulfillment that forms the vision of the

Christian leader. The new creation encompasses the entire created order and forces us beyond provincialism, exclusivity, and homogeneity.

At the heart of Wesleyan theology is universal grace available to all and working prior to our own efforts. Therefore, Methodist leaders can move beyond boundaries of ethnicity, cultures, nations, systems, religions, and fields of knowledge with confidence that God is present to create, heal, reconcile, and transform. Collaboration and partnerships across traditional boundaries become possible for those who affirm God's universal power and presence. In the pluralistic and diverse world of the twenty-first century, such partnerships and collaboration characterize Christian leaders anchored in a vision of God's salvation made possible through grace.

The shaping of evangelistic communities of grace is required of Christian leaders in the contemporary world. While the need for individuals who provide direction for institutions remains, more attention to the formation of the corporate leadership of the church and its institutions is needed. Shaping congregations that influence neighborhoods and cities requires special skill in institutional development and community organization. Creating and fostering caring communities of witness, justice, generosity, compassion, peace, and hope is necessary if the church is to be a sign, foretaste, and instrument of God's present and coming reign in both the seats of power and on the margins.

Relationships can be means of evangelism to facilitate the Christian discipleship of individuals as they are initiated into the body of Christ. Forming small groups in which people are held in love and held accountable for grow-ing in grace is an essential practice for making disciples for the transformation of the world. Additionally, communities of faith can nurture relationships across boundaries of difference including race, ethnicity, language, gender, class, education, and ability. Nurturing such communities of grace requires careful attention to group dynamics and planning and leading worship that is truly liturgical—"the work of the people" in the church and the world.

Reconciliation and conflict resolution skills are necessary for leadership in the contemporary world. God's holistic salvation includes the reconciliation of all things and the removal of barriers within the human family. As a sign and instrument of God's reconciliation, the church—local congregations, judicatories, and institutions—must confront conflicts, differences, and divisions with grace. The breaking down of homogeneity and the practice of radical hospitality require such intentional initiatives as multicultural education and sensitivity training; intentional experiences and friendship with people who are different from ourselves, particularly those on the margins; and engagement in global mission.

Leaders in the midst of diversity and polarization see conflict as an opportunity for reconciliation and growth in love of God and neighbor. Such a stance toward conflict requires a nondefensiveness born of self-awareness rooted in grace, a vision of community formed by reconciliation in Christ, and learned skills in facilitating communication in the midst of anger and frustration. The church is strategically positioned to counter destructive polarizations of violence, alienation, and retribution with a community of forgiveness, reconciliation, restoration, and transformation. Meeting this challenge requires individual and corporate leadership formed and sustained by God's presence and power at work in community.

Conclusion

Charles Dickens's classic *A Tale of Two Cities* (1859) is set in the late eighteenth century. Chapter 1 opens with these oft-quoted words:

> *It was the best of times, it was the worst of times, it was the age of wisdom, it was the age of foolishness, it was the epoch of belief, it was the epoch of incredulity, it was the season of Light, it was the season of Darkness, it was the spring of hope, it was the winter of despair, we had everything before us, we had nothing before us, we were all going direct to Heaven, we were all going direct the other way— in short, the period was so far like the present period, that some of its noisiest authorities insisted on its being received, for good or for evil, in the superlative degree of comparison only.*[9]

The description characterized eighteenth-century England and Europe, the context in which the Methodist movement was born and nurtured by John Wesley. It also resonates with the realities, challenges, and opportunities of the early years of the twenty-first century. We do live in a time of ambiguity— wisdom and foolishness, light and darkness, hope and despair, abundance and scarcity, promising vision and wrong direction.

But the church was born in such a time and has been sustained over the centuries amid multiple challenges and threats. Leaders in every age have confronted the challenges as opportunities for the manifestation of God's power and presence. The God who transformed crucifixion into resurrection in Jesus Christ is present through the Holy Spirit to bring healing, forgiveness, reconciliation, and transformation in the world of the new century.

Whether the future will be the worst of times or the best of times, as heirs of John Wesley, we know above all else that "the best of all, God is with us."

Questions for Reflection and Discussion

1. Which of the challenges/opportunities in this chapter are you confronted with in your particular context? What other challenges do you face and what opportunities arise from these challenges?

2. In your own words, what message of salvation does our modern world need? How can Christian practices and steadfast faith in God's grace help Christian leaders use their position and skills to advance God's reign in the modern world?

3. How does a "survival mentality" obscure and go against Christian understanding of salvation by grace and God's mission? How can a Christian leader redirect a community away from this mentality?

4. What dangers for the Christian leader lie in an emphasis on individualism? How does John Wesley's emphasis on mutuality and shared responsibility help the Christian leader resist individualism? What are some aspects of individualism that should be maintained by the Christian community?

5. Do you see opportunities for recovering early Methodist organization and practices (class meetings, bands, General Rules, etc.) in your particular context? If so, what and how would they need to change for present-day culture while remaining faithful to the overarching vision of God's grace and mission?

6. Identify some pressing or potential adaptive challenges in your particular context. What sort of "cultural shift" is required? What resources will you and your Christian community need in order to make such a shift on both personal and communal levels?

Conclusion

Leadership as Call and Gift

Leadership as Discipleship

In the Wesleyan tradition, grace sustains Christian leadership and discipleship. One's acceptance of God's unconditional love in Jesus Christ through the Holy Spirit is the foundation for Christian discipleship, as well as for leadership. Leadership is not limited to the execution of tasks or attainment of skills when responsibly managing large institutions. Rather, it is a way of being in relationship with God and others. Similar to discipleship, Christian leadership is both call and gift for those baptized in the name of the triune God.

Through baptism, we are invited to share in God's grace and mission for the transformation of the world. As individuals and the church universal, we are called, inspired, sanctified, and led by the Holy Spirit to participate in God's reign and mission in the world. Without this foundation in Christian doctrine, leadership—and discipleship—loses its *telos* and substance. As human beings created by God, we are invited to receive the gift of grace and to be called into relationship with God and all of creation.

For most of us, relationships, even with the Divine, require attention and cultivation. While we do not earn God's grace through Christian practices such as prayer, biblical study, and serving our neighbor, these practices can serve as means of God's grace and free us for Christian leadership. Christian practices remind us of our purpose as disciples, forming and sustaining us in God's grace. Christian communities of mutual accountability are an essential aspect of sustaining grace-filled Christian discipleship and leadership.

Who would have dreamed that a few Oxford University students in eighteenth-century England would ignite a flame of spiritual renewal that continues to burn in the twenty-first century and has now spread across the globe? The remarkable fruitfulness of the early Methodists stands as historic witness to grace, the power and presence of God to transform life. Before *leadership* entered the Methodist lexicon, John and Charles Wesley practiced it, and they provided a model of leadership formed and sustained by grace.

The denominations that claim the Wesleyan lineage in the twenty-first century seek spiritual renewal and increased fruitfulness. As beneficiaries of and successors to the leadership of the Wesleys, we are committed to identifying, calling forth, forming, deploying, and sustaining faithful participants in God's mission of salvation. The challenges to the *missio Dei* are formidable, but so are the opportunities.

Our Wesleyan tradition provides us with rich resources on which to draw and a firm foundation on which to build. The primary foundation and resource is *grace*—God's presence and power that claims and calls us as beloved children of God, redeemed in Jesus Christ, incorporated into the new creation, and sent forth to participate in God's present and coming reign of compassion, justice, generosity, and peace. Charles Wesley declared the leadership task of Methodists of all ages:

> *To serve the present age,*
> *my calling to fulfill;*
> *O may it all my powers engage*
> *to do my Master's will.*[1]

Nurturing Grace-Formed Leaders

The good news is that the one who calls us to serve the present age also equips us to do so. Through the Holy Spirit, we are formed as leaders who embody grace and used as means of grace in the church and in the world. The marks of leaders formed by grace include the following:

- steadfast focus on the triune God and a deep understanding of and formation in Scripture and the Christian tradition
- formation in doctrine, theology, and mission through continuous theological reflection and appropriating the gospel in contemporary contexts
- passionate sense of vocational calling to share in the *missio Dei*
- comprehensive vision of holistic salvation and God's present and coming reign brought near in Jesus Christ
- hope grounded in God's victory in the Cross and Resurrection over the powers of sin and death
- identity as a beloved child of God bearing the *imago Dei* and redeemed in Jesus Christ through the Holy Spirit
- self-awareness, with honest confession of failures and growth through mistakes and inadequacies
- courage to venture beyond the familiar and comfortable and into places of suffering, injustice, and marginalization
- participation in disciplined practices of holiness of heart and life within communities of support and accountability
- generosity of spirit and resources through friendships with people on the margins, especially the poor, the imprisoned, and the vulnerable

At the core of leadership formed and sustained by grace is covenant. The triune God has entered into covenant with us; and the grace to lead requires persistent renewal of our covenant with God. The early Methodists renewed their covenant at least annually with the following prayer, with which we conclude:

> *I am no longer my own, but thine.*
> *Put me to what thou wilt, rank me with whom thou wilt.*
> *Put me to doing, put me to suffering.*
> *Let me be employed by thee or laid aside for thee,*
> *exalted for thee or brought low for thee.*
> *Let me be full, let me be empty.*
> *Let me have all things, let me have nothing.*
> *I freely and heartily yield all things*
> *to thy pleasure and disposal.*
> *And now, O glorious and blessed God,*
> *Father, Son, and Holy Spirit,*

thou art mine, and I am thine. So be it.
And the covenant which I have made on earth,
let it be ratified in heaven. Amen.[2]

Questions for Reflection and Discussion

1. What marks of leadership in the Wesleyan tradition do you consider most evident and most needed today?

2. What role does *covenant* play in the formation and sustaining of leadership, and how would being part of a covenant group enhance your leadership?

Notes

Introduction

1. John Wesley, "The Witness of the Spirit," in *The Bicentennial Edition of the Works of John Wesley* (Nashville: Abingdon Press, 1976–), 1:309–10.

2. John Wesley, "Notes on Several Occasions to John Wesley's Large Minutes, in *The Works of John Wesley*, ed. T. Jackson (1892; repr. Grand Rapids: Zondervan, 1892), 8:300.

3. Charles Wesley, "Forth in Thy Name, O Lord, I Go" (1749).

Chapter 1: Christian Leadership Grounded in Doctrine and Mission

1. John Wesley, "On Living without God," *The Bicentennial Edition of the Works of John Wesley* (Nashville: Abingdon Press, 1976–), 4:171–2 (hereafter *Works*); Parker J. Palmer, *Leading from Within: Reflections on Spirituality and Leadership* (Washington, D.C.: The Servant Leadership School, 1990). This volume is a transcript of an address by Parker J. Palmer given at the Annual Celebration of the Indiana Office for Campus Ministries, March 1990.

2. William J. Abraham, *The Logic of Evangelism* (Grand Rapids: Eerdmans, 1989), 9.

3. "Doctrinal Standards and Our Theological Task," in *The Book of Discipline of The United Methodist Church—2008* (Nashville: Abingdon Press, 2008), ¶104, pp. 74–75.

4. Thomas A. Langford, "Conciliar Theology: A Report," *Quarterly Review* 9/2 (Summer 1989):9.

5. Randy L. Maddox, "Formation and Reflection: The Dynamics of Theology in Christian Life," *Quarterly Review* 21/1 (Spring 2001):22.

6. Ibid.

7. John Wesley, "A Plain Account of the People Called Methodists," in *Works*, 9:254.

8. Ibid., 254–55.

9. John Wesley, "The Scripture Way of Salvation," in *Works*, 2:156, 158.

10. John Wesley, "Farther Appeal to Men of Reason and Religion," in *Works*, 9:106.

11. A reference to Wesley's letter to the Reverend Mr. Perronet, vicar of Shoreham, written in 1748 and published as "A Plain Account of the People Called Methodists." The text of this letter can be viewed on the Web site BibleExplore.com, at http://www .god rules.net/library/wesley/274wesley_h6.htm.

12. John Wesley, "Salvation by Faith," in *Works*, 1:121.

13. "Letter to Samuel Walker, September 19, 1757," in *The Letters of John Wesley*, ed. John Telford (London: Epworth Press, 1931), 3:222.

14. "Letter to Alexander Knox, October 26, 1778," in *The Letters of John Wesley*, 6:327.

15. John Wesley, "Address to the Clergy," *The Works of John Wesley* (Grand Rapids: Zondervan, 1958), 10:468–69.

16. John Wesley, "Preface to *Hymns and Sacred Poems*, 1739," in *The Works of John Wesley* (Grand Rapids: Zondervan, 1958), 14:321.

17. John Wesley, "Sermon on the Mount, IV," in *Works*, 1:533–34.

18. John Wesley, "The "Character of a Methodist," in *Works*, 9:41.

19. John Wesley, "The New Creation," in *Works*, 2:504, 508, 509.

20. Bruce E. Winston, "Towards a Deeper Understanding of Hope and Leadership," *Journal of Leadership and Organizational Studies* (22 December 2005): 11–12.

Chapter 2: Leadership Formed by Grace

1. See Parker J. Palmer's *Let Your Life Speak: Listening for the Voice of Vocation* (San Francisco: Jossey-Bass, 1999); and *A Hidden Wholeness: The Journey toward an Undivided Life* (San Francisco: Jossey-Bass, 2004).

2. Richard P. Heitzenrater, *Wesley and the People Called Methodists* (Nashville: Abingdon Press, 1995), 27.

3. Ibid.

4. Richard P. Heitzenrater, *The Elusive Mr. Wesley: John Wesley His Own Biographer* (Nashville: Abingdon Press, 1984), 1:37.

5. Heitzenrater, *Wesley and the People Called Methodists*, 26.

6. Ibid., 27.

7. Ibid., 35.

8. Ibid., 35–36.

9. Heitzenrater, *The Elusive Mr. Wesley*, 1:50.

10. Heitzenrater, *Wesley and the People Called Methodists*, 56–58.

11. Ibid., 58–59.

12. Ibid., 61–62, 67–68. From 1743, John Wesley demonstrated his opposition to slavery, including the following statement in the General Rules for the United Societies: He prohibited "the buying or selling the bodies and souls of men, women, and children, with an intention to enslave them." Wesley also wrote on the subject in 1774, *Thoughts upon Slavery*, outlining his opposition to the practice. The last letter Wesley penned was to the British antislavery leader William Wilberforce, expressing his support: "O be not weary of well doing! Go on, in the name of God and in the power of his might, till even American slavery (the vilest that ever saw the sun) shall vanish away before it" (1791) (http:gbgm-umc.org/umw/wesley/wilber.stm).

13. Heitzenrater, *Wesley and the People Called Methodists*, 69–70, 70–71.

14. Heitzenrater, *The Elusive Mr. Wesley*, 1:38–43.

15. Ibid.

16. Heitzenrater, *Wesley and the People Called Methodists*, 77.

17. Ibid.

18. Ibid., 78–79.

19. Ibid., 79–80.

20. *Journal and Diaries*, 18:249–50; quoted in ibid., 80.

21. Heitzenrater, *Wesley and the People Called Methodists*, 80.

22. *Journal and Diaries*, 18:226; quoted in ibid., 77.

23. Heitzenrater, *Wesley and the People Called Methodists*, 98.

24. For further discussion, see Randy L. Maddox, *Responsible Grace: John Wesley's Practical Theology* (Nashville: Abingdon Press, 1994).

25. For further discussion of Wesley's treatment of sanctification and Christian perfection, see Maddox, *Responsible Grace*, especially pages 171–91.

26. From John Wesley's "Nature, Design, and General Rules of the United Societies, in London, Bristol, Kingswood, Newcastle-upon-Tyne, Etc.," or simply "The General Rules" (rule #2). The full text of the General Rules can be found in Kevin Watson, *A Blueprint for Discipleship: Wesley's General Rules as a Guide for Christian Living* (Nashville: Discipleship Resources, 2009), appendix A. Text also available on the BibleExplore Web site, at http://www.godrules.net/library/wesley/274wesley_h7.htm.

27. Jim Collins, *Good to Great: Why Some Companies Make the Leap . . . and Others Don't* (New York: HarperBusiness, 2001).

28. A constant theme in the sermons and hymns of John Wesley. For more on this topic, see Charles Yrigoyen Jr., *John Wesley: Holiness of Heart and Life* (with a study guide by Ruth A. Daugherty) (Nashville: Abingdon, 1996).

29. Stephen R. Covey, *The 7 Habits of Highly Successful People: Powerful Lessons in Personal Change* (New York: Fireside, 1989).

30. Patrick M. Lencioni, *The Five Temptations of a CEO: A Leadership Fable* (San Francisco: Jossey-Bass, 1998).

31. Sean Tucker, Nick Turner, Julian Barling, Erin M. Reid, and Cecilia Elving, "Apologies and Transformational Leadership," *Journal of Business Ethics* 63 (January 2006): 195–207.

32. Quoted in Heitzenrater, *Wesley and the People Called Methodists*, 308.

Chapter 3: Christian Leadership Sustained by Practices

1. Randy L. Maddox, "Formation for Christian Leadership: Wesleyan Reflections," *American Theological Library Association Summary of Proceedings* 57 (2003): 114–26, 115.

2. Ibid., 116. Maddox goes on to unpack the twofold natures of sin, grace, and salvation in this instructive essay.

3. See Robert L. Wilken, *Remembering the Christian Past* (Grand Rapids: Eerdmans, 1995), 124.

4. See Philip D. Kenneson, *Life on the Vine: Cultivating the Fruit of the Spirit in the Christian Community* (Downers Grove, IL: InterVarsity, 1999); and Brad J. Kallenberg, *Live to Tell: Evangelism for a Postmodern Age* (Grand Rapids: Brazos Press, 2002).

5. John Wesley, "Sermon on the Mount IV," in *Works* 1:533–34, referred to in Maddox, "Formation for Christian Leadership," 124.

6. "A Plain Account of the People Called Methodists," *Works*, 9:257; and see "Rules of the United Societies," *Works*, 8:269–71.

7. Richard P. Heitzenrater, *Wesley and the People Called Methodists* (Nashville: Abingdon Press, 1995), 21. The Society for Promoting Christian Knowledge has its roots in the religious societies founded by Anthony Horneck in the 1670s, the English counterparts to the *collegia pietatis* organized by Jacob Spener.

8. "A Plain Account of the People Called Methodists," *Works*, 9:254–80.

9. See also "Rules of the United Societies," *Works*, 8:269–71.

10. The General Rules were meant for mutual support, but were also enforced, serving as a guide for accountability specifically in the Newcastle societies of 1743. The General Rules are protected as formal doctrine within the UMC tradition and appear in the UMC Discipline. "General Rules of United Societies," *The Book of Discipline of The United Methodist Church—2008* (Nashville: The United Methodist Publishing House, 2008), 72–74.

11. Richard P. Heitzenrater, *The Elusive Mr. Wesley* (Nashville: Abingdon Press, 1984), 1:58. The questions on page 60 represent a selection of questions John Wesley used sometimes hourly to assess his spiritual demeanor. The list was begun in 1730 and expanded and altered.

12. Maddox, "Formation for Christian Leadership," 122. See also "Means of Grace," *Works*, 1:376–97.

13. Covenant discipleship is a contemporary expression of the early Wesleyan practices of the means of grace. Helpful resources are available through the General Board of

Discipleship. See especially Steven W. Manskar, *Accountable Discipleship: Living in God's Household* (Nashville: Discipleship Resources, 2000). Additionally, the Orders of Deacons and Elders offer an opportunity for accountability, holy conferencing, and Christian friendship.

14. John and Sylvia Ronsvalle, *Behind the Stained Glass Windows: Money Dynamics in the Church* (Grand Rapids: Baker Publishing Group, 1996). The Ronsvalle study surveyed twenty-nine Protestant denominations in the United States for statistics and practices from 1968 to 1995.

15. For example, see Marva J. Dawn, *Reaching Out without Dumbing Down: A Theology of Worship for This Urgent Time* (Grand Rapids: Eerdmans, 1995), particularly 2–16; and Bishop Ken Carder, "Market and Mission: Competing Visions for Transforming Ministry" (Hickman Lectures, Duke Divinity School, October 2001).

16. James S. Hewitt, *Adult Bible Studies Teacher* (Nashville: Cokesbury, 1988). See also Sondra Ely Wheeler, *Wealth as Peril and Obligation: The New Testament on Possessions* (Grand Rapids: Eerdmans, 1995).

17. Randy L. Maddox, "'Visit the Poor': John Wesley, the Poor, and the Sanctification of Believers," in *The Poor and the People Called Methodists*, ed. Richard P. Heitzenrater (Nashville: Kingswood Books, 2002), 62.

18. John Wesley, "The Use of Money," *Works*, 2:278–79.

19. Maddox, "'Visit the Poor,'" 62.

20. Ibid., 62–63.

21. Ted A. Campbell, "The Image of Christ in the Poor: On the Medieval Roots of the Wesleys' Ministry with the Poor," in *The Poor and the People Called Methodists*, 53–54; quoted from Sermon 131, "The Danger of Increasing Riches," in *Works*, 4:184.

22. John Wesley, "The Good Steward," in *Works*, 2:295.

23. Heitzenrater, *Wesley and the People Called Methodists*, 321.

24. Heitzenrater, "The Poor and the People Called Methodists," in *The Poor and the People Called Methodists*, 32, 34.

25. *The Letters of John Wesley*, 6:208–9; quoted in Heitzenrater, *Wesley and the People Called Methodists*, 252.

26. Heitzenrater, "The Poor and the People Called Methodists," 36.

27. "A Plain Account of the People Called Methodists," in *Works*, 9:277.

28. Heitzenrater, *Wesley and the People Called Methodists*, 321.

29. José Míguez Bonino, "'The Poor Will Always Be with You': Can Wesley Help Us Discover How Best to Serve 'Our Poor' Today?" in *The Poor and the People Called Methodists*, 184.

30. Heitzenrater, "The Poor and the People Called Methodists," 30. An interesting note: when John Wesley married, he greatly relaxed his stance on accumulation.

31. John Wesley's will specified that his body was to be carried to the grave by six

paupers, who were paid one pound each, and the draperies for the chapel were to be remade into dresses for the poor women of London. (Heitzenrater, *Wesley and the People Called Methodists*, 310–11).

32. Scott J. Jones, *Evangelistic Love of God and Neighbor: A Theology of Witness and Discipleship* (Nashville: Abingdon Press, 2003), 41–42. This focus on similar demographics can echo church-growth techniques based on a homogenous unit principle.

33. Heitzenrater, *Wesley and the People Called Methodists*, 97. As Heitzenrater explains, Bristol was a growing industrial center and port of nearly 50,000, about one-tenth the population of London (98–99).

34. Ibid., 98, 99; John Wesley, entry for March 29, 1739, *Journal of the Rev. John Wesley*, vol. 1 (London: J. Kershaw, 1827), 177.

35. Heitzenrater, *Wesley and the People Called Methodists*, 98–99.

36. Ibid., 100. Presumably, these field preachers felt some need to justify their irregular practice, leading to the emphasis upon such staggering numbers.

37. Ibid., 99–100. According to Heitzenrater, John Wesley suggested, "To avoid giving needless offense, we never preach *without* doors when we can with any conveniency preach *within*." The expansion was to be gradual, to "go a little and a little" from the society meetings "so a little leaven would spread with more effect and less noise, and help would always be at hand" (*Minutes*, 23).

38. Heitzenrater, *Wesley and the People Called Methodists*, 149.

39. William J. Abraham, *The Logic of Evangelism* (Grand Rapids: Eerdmans, 1989), 54–55.

40. Theodore Runyon, *The New Creation: John Wesley's Theology Today* (Nashville: Abingdon Press, 1998), 115. Runyon argues that despite George Whitefield's larger crowds and greater public attention, Wesley and his religious societies most likely preserved more fruit from the eighteenth-century revival preaching as a result of their Christian nurture and discipleship.

41. Heitzenrater, *Wesley and the People Called Methodists*, 165. John Wesley noted in the *Minutes*: "Almost all the seed has fallen by the wayside; there is scarce any fruit of it remaining." According to Heitzenrater, quoting John, "The preacher had little opportunity for instructions, the awakened souls could not 'watch over one another in love,' and the believers could not 'build up one another and bear one another's burdens'" (ibid.).

Chapter 4: Contemporary Challenges and Opportunities

1. "Minutes of Several Conversations," Q.3, in *The Works of John Wesley*, vol. 8, ed. T. Jackson (Grand Rapids: Baker, 1978), 299.

2. Bishop Kenneth L. Carder, quoted in Kathy Gilbert, "Bishops Say God Is Calling Church to a New Future," *Global Ministries* (an online publication of The United Methodist Church), April 28, 2004, http://gbgm-umc.org/global_news/full_article.cfm?articleid=2371.

3. For example, see Bryan P. Stone, *Evangelism after Christendom: The Theology and Practice of Christian Witness* (Grand Rapids: Brazos Press, 2007).

4. Quoted by Hendrik R. Pieterse in a paper delivered at the 2007 Oxford Institute for Theological Studies and published by the General Board of Higher Education and Ministry in a monogram titled *Opting for the Margins, Again: Recovering an Episcopal Initiative* (Nashville: General Board of Higher Education and Ministry, The United Methodist Church, 2007). The quote is from Charles H. Bayer, *A Resurrected Church: Christianity after the Death of Christendom* (St. Louis: Chalice Press, 2001), 2.

5. Pieterse, *Opting for the Margins*, 3.

6. Stanley Hauerwas has been in the forefront of interpreting the church's mission in terms of its identity as an alternative community. Earlier books coauthored by Hauerwas and William H. Willimon put the image clearly on the theological and ecclesial agenda. See *Resident Aliens* (Nashville: Abingdon Press, 1989) and *Where Resident Aliens Live: Exercises for Christian Practice* (Nashville: Abingdon Press, 1996).

7. Robert D. Putnam, *Bowling Alone: The Collapse and Revival of American Community* (New York: Simon and Schuster, 2000).

8. Ronald A. Heifetz, *Leadership without Easy Answers* (Cambridge, MA: The Belknap Press of Harvard University Press, 1994).

9. Charles Dickens, *A Tale of Two Cities* (London: Penguin, 2007).

Conclusion: Leadership as Call and Gift

1. Charles Wesley, "A Charge to Keep I Have," *United Methodist Hymnal* (Nashville: The United Methodist Publishing House, 1989), no. 413.

2. John Wesley, "A Covenant Prayer in the Wesleyan Tradition," *United Methodist Hymnal* (Nashville: Abingdon Press, 1989), no. 607.

CPSIA information can be obtained at www.ICGtesting.com
Printed in the USA
LVOW041250190512

282419LV00001B/82/P

9 780938 162766